HOLD YE FRONT PAGE II

21 billion years of pre-history in

By John Perry and Neil Roberts

Contents

Foreword

SUSPENSION of disbelief is the key to appreciating Hold Ye Front Page 2.

In the next 128 pages we will ask you to accept The Sun as an ethereal observer of the pivotal events in our history — from BEFORE the creation of the universe, through the dominance of the dinosaurs and the evolution of mankind to the night before Jesus Christ's birth.

In showing how The Sun might have covered these great stories we have taken an unforgivable number of liberties, more so even than in our first book, Hold Ye Front Page.

For while that dealt with the last 2,000 years, much of it well documented, hard evidence is more difficult to come by when dealing with prehistory — that is, the vast period before the invention of writing.

However, while the spoof Sun "splashes" on our right-hand pages required a certain amount of imagination, we have again attempted to provide on the left-hand pages a reliable guide to the historical evidence for each event.

We have had to make some tough choices, particularly when science and religion are in conflict.

For example we have opted to cover the Big Bang theory of the creation of the universe rather than the Adam and Eve story from the book of Genesis. And we sincerely apologise to all those who believe in the latter. We HAVE covered a few Old Testament episodes and a few ancient myths, partly because they make great stories but also because we thought

Best-seller . . . our first book, Hold Ye Front Page

it useful and interesting to place them in a historical context. For example, whether or not you believe in Noah, the story of the flood CAN be linked with an immense natural disaster for which there is sound evidence.

Once again, we make no claim for our story selection being the definitive guide to the most important events of all time — though some are indisputably so. The invention of beer, for example. Similarly we would warn you that the cross-references on the right-hand pages are more often than not for added authenticity rather than pointing you somewhere useful.

And finally, a short word about dating, since there won't be another opportunity. Historians often disagree on when prehistoric events took place, varying by hundreds or even thousands of years.

In those cases we have placed the event somewhere in the range they all accept and normally towards the date that the majority hold to be accurate.

It's also worth knowing that with ancient artefacts, bones and fossils there are scientific methods by which dates are arrived at. In a nutshell they involve measuring how much certain chemical elements in an object have decayed over time. Radiocarbon dating is good up to 50,000 years, thorium decay for 100,000 to 500,000 years, decay of potassium-40 to argon-40 for 500,000 to millions of years and decay of rubidium to strontium for billions of years. We hope that's clear.

Words, ideas and research......... **JOHN PERRY & NEIL ROBERTS**
Design .... **PHIL LEACH**

Picture Research...**HOLLY WHITELAW**
Photos...**STEVE LEWIS**
Page-building...**EMMA HOLDER**
Cartoons..**TED ANDREWS & DAVE GASKILL**
Graphics...**KATHRYN GEORGE & ROY COOPER**

7,830,155,888,390 DAYS TO GO

21,000,000,000 BC

BEFORE THE BIG BANG

IT is, of course, impossible to know what existed before the Big Bang. The various theories are pure speculation — and since they cannot be tested or proven they are philosophy rather than science.

Even though cosmologists can be fairly certain of events a few seconds after the Big Bang, they will probably never know what preceded it.

While most scientists agree that an unimaginably huge explosion "created the universe" somewhere between 13billion and 20billion years ago, there is no particular reason either to support or refute the idea that anything existed before it.

The theories are affected by whether you believe the universe to be finite (closed) or infinite (open).

It is known to be expanding at a fantastic rate, and it therefore follows that billions of years ago it was far, far smaller.

In fact, it is possible that at the moment before the Big Bang the universe was infinitely small, with all the galaxies we now know massively condensed into a space tinier than a quark — the smallest particle of matter known to man.

The distance between two points was zero, as was the volume of the entire universe, while the density of matter was infinitely great.

Some believers in a finite universe think that this infinitesimally small state was reached after a "Big Crunch" during which the previous form of our universe contracted, with galaxies, stars and planets compacting with incredible violence and temperatures of billions of degrees.

They believe that may once again be the fate of our universe 30billion years from now — and that the universe is "pulsating", expanding and contracting every 80billion years.

For the "Big Crunch" to happen again, though, the combined gravity of all the mass in the universe will have to overcome the speed at which the galaxies are expanding. Other scientists, even those who believe in the closed universe, dismiss this theory, believing there is not enough mass to halt the expansion. Some experts believe the universe is infinite and will expand forever.

The fact is that the question of existence before the Big Bang may well be meaningless, because in trying to make sense of it the human mind is limited to concepts which the Big Bang actually created. Our imaginations cannot cope without thinking of things in terms of space, time, gravity, energy and matter. And yet the chances are that, before the Big Bang, none of those existed.

Wednesday, October 11, 21452481886BC

THOUGHT: STILL NOTHING

MORE NOTHINGNESS: PAGES 4 & 5

14.5bn BC

BIG BANG AND THE FORMATION OF EARTH

THE Big Bang is the theory, accepted by almost all scientists, of how the universe was created. It involves an explosion of unimaginable size, some time between 13billion and 20billion years ago, which created time and space and has resulted ever since in the universe expanding at a tremendous rate.

Originally based on equations contained in Albert Einstein's 1915 theory of relativity, the Big Bang theory has been expanded and given weight by scientists ever since.

Notable among them was the American astronomer Edwin Hubble who proved for the first time in 1929 that galaxies were moving away from each other — a phenomenon provable through "redshift", a change in the light given off by an object.

Scientists in the 1940s predicted that "cosmic background radiation" from the Big Bang should still exist — and their successors in 1965 detected it.

The theory is as follows: At the moment before the Big Bang the universe was infinitely small and infinitely dense (see Page 4). In the microseconds after the explosion, the universe expanded at an enormous rate. It has been estimated that its size increased by 100,000,000,000,000,000, 000,000,000,000,000,000,000,000, 000,000 times in 0.0000000000000000 0000000000000001 of a second. Then the expansion rate slowed to something like what it is now.

The universe cooled as it expanded. After about a second, protons formed and within a few minutes they mixed with neutrons to form basic elements.

From about 300,000 to about one million years after the Big Bang, the universe cooled to about 3000°C (about 5000°F).

For billions of years after that the universe consisted solely of vast swirling clouds of gas and dust. The first stars gradually formed at the centres of these spinning clouds, as gravity condensed them and their immense temperature ignited nuclear fusion reactions within them. Planets were made in the same way. The star-forming process continues today.

Galaxies, made up of hundreds of millions of stars each, began to form.

It has been estimated that there are now 125billion galaxies in the universe. All the stars visible to the naked eye from Earth belong to our galaxy, the Milky Way. Our sun is just one of those stars.

The Hubble Telescope, however, has brought pictures of other galaxies, some of them among the earliest in the universe and dating back around 12billion years. The light from them has taken 12billion years to reach the Hubble and has therefore crossed most of the universe. That's about 70,388,352,000,000,000,000,000 miles (roughly 70 sextillion miles).

By comparison, our Milky Way is

 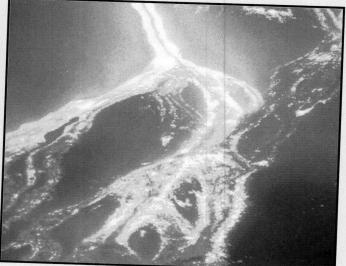

Left, a picture taken by the Hubble Space Telescope in 1998 of the furthest point ever seen in the universe — some of the galaxies here are 12billion light years away. Right, lava flow from Mount Etna in Sicily — the early Earth was a mass of volcanic eruptions

thought to be only about 100,000 light years across (that is 100,000 times the distance light travels in a year at its accepted speed of 186,000 miles a second — 586,569,600,000,000,000 miles, roughly 586 quadrillion miles).

Intriguingly, it is estimated that up to 99 per cent of all the matter in the universe is invisible and undetectable by human science. This "dark matter" is the only way scientists can explain enormous gravitational forces which influence the movement of galaxies but the source of which cannot be traced.

The Earth was formed 4.6billion years ago, ten billion years or so after the Big Bang and at about the time the sun

reached its current size. The planet melted due to radioactivity and the continuous contraction of its elements. Heavier ones like iron and nickel sunk towards the centre, forming Earth's core, while lighter ones formed the mantle (which is still molten) and the crust, which cooled and became rocky plates floating on the surface.

The Earth was also subject at this stage to "accretion" — constant bombardment by debris from space. The planet surface was a mass of volcanic activity which gave off carbon dioxide and nitrogen. Water vapour condensed to form the oceans.

Methane, which was also present,

was turned by water and sunlight into carbon dioxide, while water broke up into hydrogen and oxygen. The hydrogen left Earth's atmosphere, but a low level of oxygen remained.

The atmosphere had high levels of carbon dioxide and ammonia and the Earth had no ozone layer protecting it from the sun's ultraviolet rays. Until, that is, the first life evolved — capable of existing without much oxygen or ozone protection.

Those first life forms, through photosynthesis (see Page 8), turned the atmosphere into what we have today — nitrogen (78%), oxygen (20.95%), argon (0.93%), water (0 to 4%) and carbon dioxide (0.0325%).

ADAM AND EVE

ADAM and Eve were the first man and woman and the ancestors of the entire human race, according to the Old Testament.

The book of Genesis tells how God created Adam from dust. Eve was then created from Adam's rib and became his wife.

The couple lived together in the earthly paradise of the Garden of Eden. They were told they could eat the fruit of every tree in the garden, except the tree of knowledge.

But Eve was visited by the devil, in the form of a snake, and persuaded to eat an apple from the tree of knowledge. She then gave the apple to Adam,

who also ate it. The Bible says Adam and Eve immediately lost their innocence. Realising for the first time they were naked, they hurried to cover themselves up.

When God discovered what the couple had done they were banished from Paradise.

The Adam and Eve story is similar in many respects to the creation myths of other ancient Middle Eastern cultures, like that of the Sumerians.

Most modern Biblical scholars accept the tale is a Hebrew legend.

But some Christian fundamentalists still believe it is the true story of man's creation.

Depiction of Eve offering Adam the forbidden apple in the Garden of Eden. This painting is The Fall From Grace, by Lucas Cranach (1533)

THE Sun

Monday, November 23, 14591689406BC   THOUGHT: WATCH THIS SPACE

BANG

FULL EXPLOSIVE STORY - Page 9

1,273,074,639,804 DAYS TO GO

3.5bn BC

THE FIRST LIFE

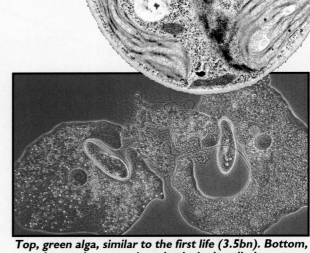

ALL life on Earth sprang from tiny single-cell organisms that emerged around 3.5billion BC. No one yet knows how they were created. Millions believe God created them.

Others believe life arrived in a cloud of dust from a passing comet, or even that it was planted on Earth by aliens.

Whether or not you believe in God, it is possible to arrive at a scientific explanation.

Producing living cells from nothing would have needed a remarkable chain of chemical events brought about by the conditions on primitive Earth.

The planet was an extremely inhospitable place by human standards. Volcanos erupted all over the surface. It was constantly hit by lightning and battered by space debris.

Earth's atmosphere had more hydrogen than oxygen. It had copious amounts of carbon dioxide, water vapour, methane and ammonia.

When the heat from the volcanos and lightning mixed with these chemicals, it produced simple organic chemicals — carbon-based chemicals essential for life.

Scientists have tested this by simulating Earth's early atmosphere in laboratories and passing sparks through it. This produces amino acids and the components of nucleic acids (DNA is a nucleic acid). Billions of years ago these chemicals are thought to have become concentrated in the lakes and tidal pools which formed as water vapour from Earth's volcanos condensed. The result was a rich primordial "soup".

It is believed that the effect of heat and the sun's ultraviolet rays condensed these simple

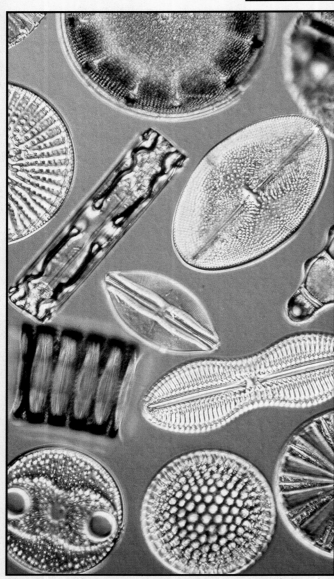

Hugely-magnified image of marine diatoms, types of algae (see 3.5bn) found in the sea. They harden into rock called diatomite

Top, green alga, similar to the first life (3.5bn). Bottom, amoebae and paramecium, both single-celled creatures

molecules into more complex ones resembling proteins and nucleic acids. Some of these must have been capable of replicating themselves. From these, the first living cells arose.

From that point, Charles Darwin's theory of natural selection kicks in. Only those cells which could adapt best to the surroundings survived.

The first cells developed into bacteria and algae, a lower form of plant life. Some of the world's oldest fossils, found in Transvaal, South Africa, and dating back 3.1billion years, have traces of both.

They were to prove crucial for the development of all other life. For they fed themselves by a process called photosynthesis, which uses the sun's energy to

produce carbohydrates from carbon dioxide and water — giving off oxygen. Over millions of years these tiny organisms transformed Earth's atmosphere into one based on nitrogen and oxygen. A layer of ozone, a form of oxygen, built up around the planet and shielded it from the sun's ultraviolet rays.

Around 1.4billion years ago, more complex cells evolved and led to more complex creatures.

Some 600million years ago the only life on Earth was still in the oceans. But the oxygen level gradually grew and sea creatures evolved, capable of breathing oxygen in the water.

By 400million years ago there was enough oxygen for animals to venture on to land and breathe the air.

...Timeline...

14.5billion The Big Bang creates the universe, which expands as matter hurtles through space.

4.6bn Earth formed — the merger of dust, gas and debris flying through space at incredible temperatures; Beginning of the Archaeozoic Era.

4.3bn Earth melts, giving off water, ammonia, nitrogen, methane, hydrogen and carbon dioxide. Ultraviolet light dissipates water into oxygen and

hydrogen. The hydrogen escapes into space, the oxygen remains.

4bn The bombardment of the Earth by debris stops.

3.8bn Earth's crust cools and hardens, forming the oldest rocks on the planet; Water in atmosphere condenses into oceans.

3.5bn Single-cell organisms such as bacteria and algae develop in sea, producing oxygen which gradually makes other life possible as well as bolstering Earth's protective ozone layer.

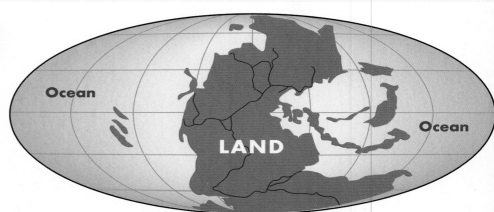

Graphic shows how after the Earth's crust hardened into rocky plates (see 3.8bn), the planet's entire land mass is thought to have been one continent now called Pangaea, surrounded by sea

THE Sun

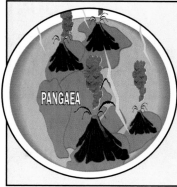

PANGAEA

Saturday, June 5, 3487875726BC — THOUGHT: SOUPER STAR

TODAY'S WEATHER

TODAY will see a continuation of the very warm weather we've been enjoying for the last billion years. Temperatures are likely to soar to a sizzling 90°C in all parts of the world. Volcanos will erupt constantly throughout the day and night. Humidity will be unbearable and the air unbreathable. Ammonia count: Very high. Pollen count: Nil. Chance of a meteorite shower: 100%. Forecast for tomorrow: Similar.

Live cells 'scattered on Earth by aliens'

By LIL GREENMAN
Space Correspondent

THE bugs now infesting Earth may have been planted here by ALIENS, it was sensationally claimed last night.

Beings from outer space with advanced intelligence are said to have peppered our oceans with the tiny organisms to see if they will grow.

They allegedly hope to return to our planet later to monitor the creatures' progress.

If the bugs eventually evolve into more complex beings, the aliens aim to abduct a few from their homes and whisk them off into space to carry out embarrassing experiments,

Alien .. did he bring bugs?

it is claimed. Each of their visits by spacecraft will be carried out with the utmost secrecy so their presence can never be proved.

Experts last night pooh-poohed the extra-terrestrial theory, saying it was concocted to dodge having to work out a scientific explanation for the development of life on Earth.

In fact, since the allegation assumes that beings already exist elsewhere in the universe, it neatly avoids the question of how life began anywhere.

Other scientists claimed yesterday that Earth's new life-forms DID come from outer space — contained in the dust from a comet.

But it was later pointed out that the intense amounts of radiation in space would kill any bugs.

LIFE: THE FIRST PICTURE

OOZE THAT IN THE SWAMP?

Riddle over bugs living in our 'soup'

By AL GEE

THIS is the shocking picture that proves tiny organisms are ALIVE on Earth.

The "bugs" have only one cell each, but are multiplying. Soon they may be out of control.

They are based in our primordial "soup" — the chemical-rich lakes and pools all over the planet.

It is a total mystery where they came from.

WORRYING

Conditions on Earth since its launch about a billion years ago have always been too unpleasant for life.

These "beings" must have used the energy from our spectacular lightning displays, and our hydrogen and ammonia-based atmosphere, to their advantage.

A Sun spokesman said last night: "This is certainly a worrying development. If these bugs manage to become multi-cellular, who knows where it will end?"

It's A Cell's Market — Page 7

Graphic shows how Earth's shifting land mass may have looked 550m years ago (top left), 500m years ago (top right), 450m years ago (above left) and 400m years ago

...Timeline...

1.4bn Organisms with more than one cell develop in sea. Beginning of Proterozoic Era.

545m Hard-bodied organisms on the rise in sea. Beginning of the Paleozoic Era (Cambrian Period).

505m Beginning of the Paleozoic Era's Ordovician Period.

500m Jellyfish, worms and coral develop.

438m First fish develop; Beginning of the Paleozoic Era's Silurian Period.

430m Some algae begin to flourish on land.

420m Arthropods (e.g. millipedes, centipedes and scorpion-like creatures) develop and leave oceans.

410m Beginning of the Paleozoic Era's Devonian Period.

400m First proper fish evolves, with skull and backbone.

395m Fish evolve jaws. Sharks up to 50ft long rule the oceans.

375m Appalachian mountains (America) formed as plates making up North America, Europe and Africa collide.

360m BC

FIRST ANIMALS ON LAND

Fossils of ammonites, some of the earliest sea creatures. They died out with dinosaurs

Fossil of a trilobite, another shelled sea creature which thrived 500m years ago

AN obscure creature called Acanthostega was responsible for a momentous step in the evolution of life on Earth.

Essentially a fish, it was nonetheless the first animal to emerge from the water and live partly on land.

The honour could equally go to Ichthyostega, but it is impossible to tell which made it first.

In 500million BC, some 140million years before Acanthostega and Ichthyostega, Earth's only animal life was the primitive creatures drifting about in the shallow seas.

They included jellyfish, sponges, shellfish, starfish, sea urchins, sea cucumbers and worms. Shelled creatures like trilobites and ammonites also thrived.

The first fish evolved 438million years ago. They had no jaws, fins or head to speak of and spent their days drifting along the seabed using their gills to strain food particles from water. Long and thin, they had a cord running from front to back which evolved in later creatures into a backbone.

By 400million BC, the first fish proper was on the scene. They still had no jaws but they had a skull, a spine and two fins.

During the Devonian period, around 395million BC, there was an explosion in fish development.

They evolved jaws which enabled them to hunt bigger prey throughout the oceans, plus improved fins for better mobility. Sharks up to 50ft long evolved.

An important transition then occurred. Lungfish emerged, with proper lungs and the ability to breathe air by rising just above the surface of the water. They also used their two sets of fins, front and back, as legs to crawl along the bottoms of rivers and lakes.

Acanthostega, which evolved around 360million BC, was an advance on that. A bizarre 4ft-long creature with a fishy tail, it had tiny arms, legs, feet and hands, each of which had eight "fingers". Meanwhile Ichthyostega, about half Acanthostega's size, had seven toes on each foot.

While these two were the first to crawl out of the water, they did little more than flop about on land. Their bodies were not evolved enough for full-time terrestrial living and they spent most of their time swimming in lagoons.

A fossil found in Scotland in 1992 may well be that of the first animal to spend its entire life on land. Twenty million years younger than Acanthostega, the six-inch-long Casineria had a stiffer backbone to support its body weight. The bones of its four limbs were better designed for walking and the five fingers on each hand had ligaments allowing them to bend.

Its smaller size is another clue. Backboned animals of this time were not yet able to eat vegetation. Their diet would have been millipedes and centipedes — which might have sustained a small creature like Casineria, but not a big one like Acanthostega.

And so, for millions of years, four-legged land animals ruled the world, developing long jaws, snouts and tongues to forage for food.

The first insects arrived in 325million BC and flying insects 25million years later. They got bigger and bigger — dragonflies could have a 2½ft wingspan. Millipedes were several feet long, cockroaches grew to four inches.

The first reptiles, the 3ft-long Cotylosaurs, emerged at the earliest 300million years ago, with short necks, stumpy legs and long tails.

Within another 70million years the first dinosaurs, thecodonts, had arrived. The size of turkeys, they were little clue to the terrifying scale of those that followed.

Millipedes like this evolved around 420m and were first creatures to leave the sea

THE Sun

3am news

Monday, January 4, 351839711BC

THOUGHT: SHAPE OF FINS TO COME

One small step for a fish, one giant leap for fishkind

THIS WAS THE HISTORIC MOMENT YESTERDAY WHEN A FISH BECAME THE FIRST ANIMAL TO WALK ON LAND. READ THE FULL STORY OF PLUCKY ACANTHOSTEGA'S AWE-INSPIRING ACHIEVEMENT ON PAGES 2, 3, 4, 5, 6 & 7

...Timeline...

355m Beginning of the Paleozoic Era's Carboniferous Period.

350m Ferns evolve — Earth's first rooted plant.

325m Insects develop. They and the arthropods grow huge.

300m Reptiles appear, as do the first flying insects.

290m Beginning of the Paleozoic Era's Permian Period.

280m Beetles and weevils make an appearance.

245m Icthyosaurs, marine reptiles, emerge in sea.

230m First dinosaurs; Mesozoic Era (Triassic Period) starts.

228m Peteinosaurus, an early pterosaur or flying reptile, appears in Europe (extinct 215m BC).

225m Bees make their first appearance.

222m 8ft predator Coelophysis appears in North America; Main predator is 18ft Postosuchus, also found in North America (both extinct 215m BC); Termites and roaches evolve.

210m Plateosaurus, 23ft leaf-eater, emerges in Europe (extinct by 195m BC).

205m Beginning of the Mesozoic Era's Jurassic Period.

200m Pangea begins to break up; Crocodiles appear, as do mammals, evolving from reptiles.

165m Biggest-ever carnivore Liopleurodon, 150-ton plesiosaur, appears (extinct 150m BC).

160m Stegosaurus appears in North America, a giant herbivore up to 40ft long (extinct 140m BC).

155m Diplodocus, 85ft-long plant-eater, appears (extinct by 145m BC).

150m Meat-eater Allosaurus appears (extinct 145m BC); Brachiosaurus, giant leaf-eater, appears in America and Tanzania (extinct 125m BC).

145m Archaeopteryx, ancestor of modern birds, appears; Compsognathus, a two-legged, scampering meat-eater the size of a goose, appears in Europe (extinct by 140m BC).

135m Beginning of the Mesozoic Era's Cretaceous Period; Appearance of 30ft-long plant-eater Iguanadon (extinct 100m BC).

120m Baryonyx, a 12ft predator, appears in Britain — only one example has been found, in Surrey.

110m 9ft carnivore Deinonychus appears (extinct 100m BC).

100m Cranes appear, as do early marsupials.

97m Velociraptor appears in Asia (extinct 66m BC).

75m Quetzalcoatlus, largest flying animal with 40ft wingspan, makes first appearance (in North America).

74m Ostrich-like Gallimimus appears (extinct 70m BC).

72m Triceratops, four-footed vegetarian with three-horned face, appears in North America.

67m Tyrannosaurus Rex appears in North America.

66m Extinction of dinosaurs; mammals gain prominence Beginning of Cenozoic Era, Tertiary Period (Paleocene Epoch).

Fossilised footprints of a two-legged dino predator in Spain

Skull of allosaurus, the huge, fearsome meat-eater (150m)

The sea reptile, icthyosaur, pre-dates dinosaurs (245m)

Leaf-eater Chasmosaurus lived in about 70m BC, this one in Canada

Skeleton of a stegosaur (160m) in rock found in Wyoming, U.S.

66m BC
DEATH OF DINOSAURS

THE most heavily-favoured of the various theories as to why the dinosaurs were wiped out around 66.4million BC is that a giant asteroid hit the Earth with catastrophic effects.

Certainly, something seems to have annihilated in one fell swoop the dinosaurs, pterosaurs (flying reptiles) plesiosaurs (sea reptiles) and a host of small sea creatures such as the ammonites. But since dating techniques going back that far have a half-million-year margin of error it is hard to be absolutely certain the extinctions were down to one sudden event.

Nonetheless the discovery of a 112-mile-wide under-sea crater off the Yucatan Peninsula of Mexico in the early 1990s lends considerable weight to the theory.

The asteroid which caused it is thought to have been 6½ miles across, weighing one quadrillion tons and hit the Earth at hundreds of thousands of miles an hour with a force 10,000 times greater than all the world's current nuclear weapons combined.

The blast wave would have gone around the globe. Any dinosaurs which survived that would have been destroyed as a cloud of dust blotted out the sun completely for months or even years, dramatically lowering the Earth's temperature. Plants would have died, as would herbivores who fed on them and the carnivores who preyed on the herbivores. No land animal larger than a modern-day dog lived.

Rocks dating from around this time, found in various parts of the world, show high levels of the metal iridium, which is rare on Earth but more common in meteorites.

Some scientists dismiss the asteroid theory, however, on the basis that the fossil evidence seems to show a gradual decline in dinosaur numbers and types rather than a sudden obliteration. There are many other theories. One states that the break-up of Pangea — the vast, single continent which contained all the Earth's land mass — caused the climate to change from warm and tropical to cooler and more seasonal.

This meant tropical plants and rainforests in which the dinosaurs thrived gave way to woodlands, to which small mammals were better suited. Another theory is that the dinosaurs were wiped out by a great plague.

So did any dinosaurs survive the extinction? Many scientists now believe they did. Birds are direct descendants of archaeopteryx (meaning "ancient wing"), a crow-sized bird with teeth which lived around 145million years ago. Its skeleton has similarities with that of the velociraptor and other predators — and it is thought they shared a common ancestor.

Therefore today's birds may well be directly descended from a small predatory dinosaur — and indeed many scientists now refer to birds as dinosaurs. Oh, and those who believe in the Loch Ness monster say it's probably descended from a Plesiosaur which miraculously survived the mass extinction in the oceans.

Other creatures definitely survived — frogs, turtles, crocodiles and, of course, mammals.

Mammals evolved at roughly the same time as the first dinosaurs and co-existed with them for many millions of years. They remained small in order to hide from the reptiles — but once the dinosaurs were gone they rose to prominence.

Within a few million years rodents evolved, then rabbits and hares.

Within another few million years the early forms of the horse and dog arrived. And 43million years after the dinosaurs disappeared, apes were on the scene.

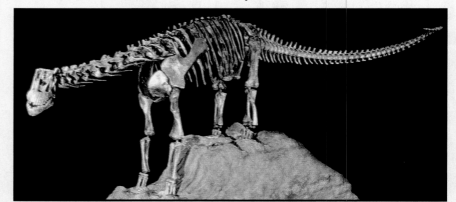
Camarasaurus, smaller relative of the giant leaf-eaters such as Diplodocus, lived until around 140m BC in North America. It was still as much as 60ft long and 18 tons

THE Sun

THEY NEVER SAUR IT COMING

See Pages 4 & 5

Wednesday, February 15, 66423892bc   THOUGHT: METEOR MAKER

Tyrannosaurus wrecks

Dinosaurs wiped out as asteroid hits Earth

By DEE PIMPACT

THE dinosaurs were wiped out last night by a gigantic asteroid.

Tyrannosaurus Rex and his fearsome pals, who have ruled the Earth for 164million years, were obliterated when the six-mile-wide chunk of rock hit the planet with incredible force.

Hundreds of thousands of dinos were killed instantly by a blast wave that went around the globe.

The rest are doomed by a giant cloud of dust which is likely to block out the sun's light and heat for months.

The extinction is terrific news for the host of small furry mammals who have been subjected to generations of terror and misery by the ferocious reptiles.

The Sun Says — Page Five

THEY NEVER SAUR

Bolt from blue ends 164m years of hel

By ARCHIE OPTERICS

THE world was last night finally freed from the tyranny of the dinosaurs who have ruled our planet through fear for 164million years.

And the killer blow came from where the reptiles least expected — **OUTER SPACE**.

Among those destroyed as the asteroid struck was the evil 39ft, six-ton Tyrannosaurus Rex — a compassionless monster which devoted its life to murder and mayhem.

Luckily we had already seen the back of the merciless Giganotosaurus, who was 2ft bigger than T-Rex and the world's biggest land predator.

The Sun predicted the threat of these "terrible lizards" when the first ones emerged in 230million BC right at the start of the Triassic period.

The first, Eoraptor and Herrerasaurus, were nasty little two-legged meat-eaters with a taste for small herbivores.

In a hard-hitting The Sun Says editorial on March 29, 230596231BC we warned that there would be more — and they would get bigger. Within a matter of a few million years, Coelophysis was on the scene — 9ft tall, incredibly light and agile and with an even more disgusting habit than its predecessors . . . it ate its **OWN** young.

After that came a beast twice the size — Postosuchus, an 18ft crocodile with legs.

And whenever one of them died out, something worse took its place.

Once we got into the Jurassic period after 193million BC, there was no stopping them.

Claws

The prey grew bigger to fight off the predators — so the predators began to evolve into giants too.

The savage Allosaurus was 15ft high, 36ft long and weighed two tons.

It had three-fingered hands with claws for ripping flesh and a skull about a metre long with 70 razor-sharp teeth.

We thought we'd seen it all. Then along came the Cretaceous period and the biggest of the lot — Giganotosaurus, a hellish 41ft creature who would run up to the giant leaf-eaters and rip out their sides.

When T-Rex came along a couple of million years ago he was almost an anti-climax by comparison — though he was crueller.

Rex used to pick up victims in his mouth and shake them violently to break every bone in their body. Only then would he eat them.

But when it came to pure evil, size very definitely did not matter.

Deinonychus, from 110million BC, was a comparative midget at only 9ft, but he would go hunting with a pack of his mates, pick on a harmless animal twice his size and tear it to shreds.

He made the Velociraptor who came shortly after him look like an enthusiastic amateur.

Other vile creatures made the giant predators seem positively noble.

Tiny, vicious Compsognathus, from 145million BC, used to scuttle around snapping up harmless lizards asleep on rocks. Back i[n] 70million BC sneaky Oviraptor used to stea[l] other dinos' eggs and scoff them. Cowardl[y] Baryonyx, from 120million BC, was 12f[t] long — but picked on **FISH**.

Even our oceans were full of killin[g] machines, all now dead.

Ichthyosaurs back in the early Triassi[c] reached an amazing 50ft.

Respect

And it was lucky that monstrous 150-to[n] Liopleurodon stuck to swimming — if he'[d] appeared on land in 160million BC he'[d] have eaten Allosauruses in one gulp.

Some dinos we'll be sorry to see go — mainly the "gentle giant" leaf-eaters of th[e] Jurassic. We'll never forget 75ft-long Baro[-] saurus or 85ft Diplodocus. Or the tiny[-] brained, 76ft and 42-ton Apatosaurus.

Or Brachiosaurus, who grew to 40ft hig[h] to reach the tops of all but the tallest tree[s]

Or the biggest dino of all time, Seismosau[rus]

IT COMING

Sinners or saints . . (main picture) evil Spinosaurus. Above, Allosaurus and Triceratops. Below, Parasaurolophus and Pterodactyl. Far right, Diplodocus.

us, the "earthquake lizard", who was an awesome 164ft long. These vegetarians earned The Sun's respect simply by being too big to attack.

If a pack of predators picked on them, they could whip the tips of their enormous tails into the attacker's face faster than the speed of sound.

Others we'll miss for their eccentricity. Some were frankly hilarious. Among those wiped out yesterday were Parasaurolophus, a leaf-eater with a hollow length of bone on his head which looks like a carrying handle.

Also gone: Pachycephalosaurus, another veggie with a huge dome of bone on his bonce which he used for butting rivals.

And Gallimimus, a tiny-headed beast like a huge, flightless bird who used to charge around everywhere at 35mph.

Extinct as of yesterday is Ankylosaurus, who built the ultimate defence against the predators – ridges of bony armour all over his back.

And there was brave, lovable Triceratops, with three horns on his head, who used to give the T-Rex a run for his money.

Last, but not least, there was the giant Stegosaurus, extinct since 140million BC, but still memorable for his armour-plating and the fearsome spiked club on the end of his tail for defence against meat-eaters.

BIRDS ARE TIPPED TO TAKE OVER

Early bird . . archaeopteryx was first

BOOKIES last night named BIRDS as hot favourites to take over the world.

Descended from the Archaeopteryx, they are swift, have the power of flight and have millions of years' experience.

Second favourites are insects, which outnumber any other creature but would need somehow to co-ordinate action.

Crocodiles are third favourites, chiefly due to their size and dinosaur-style savagery. But they're few and far between.

Sharks are outsiders — restricted, as they are, to the sea. If they can learn to colonise land, they'll be right up there.

Rank outsiders are mammals. Small, furry and harmless. A significant size increase could make them a dark horse. Odds: Birds 5-4; Insects 7-2; Crocs 4-1; Sharks 10-1; Mammals 100-1.

1,818,695,566 DAYS TO GO

5,000,000 BC

FROM APES TO MAN

MANKIND first evolved from apes as australopithecines, who, while remaining very apelike, learned to walk on two legs — a characteristic that has proved fundamental to our supremacy on Earth.

Ever since that pivotal period around five million years ago there have been various forms of "human" — several of which lived at the same time — but modern humans, classified as Homo Sapiens Sapiens, are the only ones left.

All primates — including humans, apes, monkeys, lemurs and even tree shrews — originally evolved from small mammals which began to thrive around 55million BC, ten million years after the extinction of the dinosaurs.

There were various different kinds. Some competed with rodents, and were probably driven to live in trees by the fierce competition.

By about 23million BC, some of these primitive primates had evolved into the first large apes. It is from one type of these — though scientists are unsure which — that the australopithecines sprang some 18 million years later.

"Australopithecine" means "southern ape" and refers to South Africa, where the first known australopithecine fossils were found. Indeed mankind, in the form of the australopithecines, evolved in Africa and never left that continent.

The first such creature was Australopithecus Ramidus, followed by Australopithecus Anamensis, Australopithecus Afarensis, Australopithecus Africanus, Australopithecus Boisei and Australopithecus Robustus. Scientists argue that there were other varieties too. One of the most famous Australopithecine fossils is the

This 70-yard fossilised footprint trail found in Tanzania proves that australopithecus was walking on two legs 3.6m years ago

part-complete skeleton of a female Afarensis, since nicknamed Lucy, who lived around 3.5million years ago and was discovered in Hadar, Ethiopia, in 1974. A reconstruction of Lucy is on display at London's Natural History Museum.

About 98 per cent of modern human DNA is identical with that of the chimpanzee — and indeed australopithecines were very chimp-like. They were between 3½ and 5ft tall and weighed 60 to 108lb. They were probably no brighter than an ape since their brains were about the same size.

They probably had the same facial characteristics and full covering of body hair. Their social lives were probably much like those of the chimpanzee and it is thought that since they had long arms and long, curved fingers they probably spent much of their time in trees.

Crucially, however, they walked upright, unlike the apes. Proof of this

came in 1978 when a team led by the British paleoanthropologist Mary Leakey discovered a set of footprints preserved in hardened volcanic ash at Laetoli, northern Tanzania. They date back 3.6million years, and show an apelike creature walking on two feet.

This gave australopithecus advantages over apes and allowed him to flourish. It enabled him to feed from low branches and bushes more easily than a four-legged creature. It freed his hands to carry food and to make and carry basic tools or weapons. It allowed him to peer over things to spot predators. It exposed less of him to the African sun and more to cooling winds.

All forms of australopithecus were extinct by 900,000BC at the latest. The later version, Australopithecus Robustus, co-existed with the more "human" creature, Homo Habilis, which itself evolved from an earlier australopithecine.

The reconstruction of australopithecine 'Lucy' on display in Natural History Museum, London

...Timeline...

57m Rats, mice, squirrels, storks and herons appear.

55m Rabbits and hares evolve; Beginning of Cenozoic Era's Eocene Epoch; Small mammals now thriving — some live near the sea and venture in often for food, gradually evolving into sea-dwellers like the dolphin (dolphin's ancestors once hunted the plains of Africa).

54m Ancestor of the horse, the Eohippus, appears in Europe and America — has four toes on each front foot and three each at the rear.

44m The Alps are formed.

40m Early dog appears, evolved over 20m years from a weasel-like mammal.

38m Beginning of Cenozoic Era's Oligocene Epoch.

30m Sabre-toothed tigers emerge, as do pigs; Largest-ever mammal emerges around now, the leaf-eating Indricotherium, an early rhino 18ft at the shoulder

and weighing 30 tons; Himalayas are thrown up as two land masses collide.

28m Koalas' first appearance.

26m Beginning of Cenozoic Era's Miocene Epoch.

23m Large apes appear.

20m Parrots and pigeons evolve; Chimps appear; A lush continent called the Kerguelen Plateau, a third the size of modern Australia,

sinks beneath the southern Indian Ocean.

7m Apes and hominids begin to evolve differently.

6m Beginning of Cenozoic Era's Pliocene Epoch.

5m The first variety of australopithecine appears in eastern Africa — Australopithecus Ramidus walks part-time on two legs. It co-exists with apes and later with variety of other ape-man creatures.

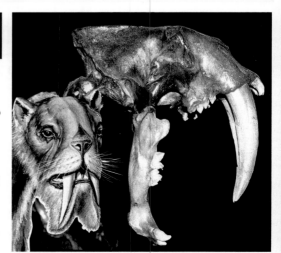

An artist's impression of a sabre-toothed tiger (evolved about 30m) and skull of the same beast

THE Sun

THOUGHT: GOODBYE CRAWL WORLD

STAND-UP COMICS

Bungling apes' barmy bid to walk 'upright'

10 things you can't do standing up

THIS "standing upright" craze is the height of stupidity — because there are some things you just can't do on two legs. Here are ten:

1 Move around: Just try taking a step. Oh dear, you seem to have fallen over!

2 Thinking. It takes all one's brain power to remain upright. Let your mind wander and CRASH!

3 Scratch your nose: The tiniest pressure on your face sends you hurtling backwards into oblivion.

4 Hide in bushes: Have a go. Hello! We can see your head poking out the top!

5 Sleep: See under Thinking for detailed explanation.

6 Go out in the wind: It's obvious if you think about it (but please don't try if you're still standing up!)

7 Hunt for grubs: By the time you've spotted them and got back on all fours to grab a gobful, the little blighters have run off.

8 Dig a hole: Ever tried to do this with a foot? Don't.

9 Sitting down. Clearly impossible — and dangerous.

10 Mating: No explanation needed.

Look mum, I'm ape-right . . . potty 'Pith takes a faltering step yesterday as his pal nurses a knee gashed when he overbalanced

CENSORED

A BIZARRE group of apes caused hilarity last night by insisting that in future they plan to stand on TWO legs.

The Australopithecines cult claim being "upright" has a string of advantages including that it frees up the hands to do other things.

But their wacky experiment immedi-

By STAN DUP and SID DOWN

ately fell flat on its face — when they kept overbalancing.

Most were unable to stand for longer than a few seconds. One, pictured in the centre above, fell awkwardly and gashed his right knee.

The "Piths", as they are nicknamed, have often been accused of elitism over their ambition to be better than normal apes. Even though they are

almost identical to chimpanzees, and no brighter, they have insisted on cutting down the amount of time they spend swinging through the trees.

Despite the fact that it is unarguably easier to balance on all-fours, they maintain that the way forward is on two feet.

They say an upright posture allows one to pick berries off trees more easily, to carry food without dragging it along the ground and to peer over objects to see predators from a dis-

tance. The Piths also claim that it will eventually lead to them being able to use tools, which most commentators believe will be a key step in the apes' evolution.

Last night a Sun spokesman said: "One has to admire their guts. Their theory flies in the face of all logic and leaves them open to ridicule.

"But credit to them, they're standing up for what they believe is right."

Falling Down Pithed — Pages 4 & 5

Fury at berry 'mountain'

TRIBAL chiefs last night sparked uproar among their apemen followers — after it was revealed they have created a huge BERRY mountain.

The chiefs have been encouraging hunter-gatherers to work extra hours picking berries so that they can be hoarded in case of famine.

But so many berries have been set aside they now make a pile as tall as the average apeman.

Many of those at the bottom of the pile have already gone soft.

One hunter-gatherer said last night: "It's a disgrace. We worked hard to collect those berries and now they're left to rot."

Trees crisis is looming

TREE overcrowding is on the rise — and will become a serious problem if alternative homes cannot be found.

In some parts of Europe it has become common to find up to FIVE families of apemen living together in one small conifer.

Last month disaster struck when two homeless families began squatting in a silver birch that was not yet mature.

Three adult apes plunged 10ft to the ground when a branch gave way under their weight. One died and the others broke bones.

Some groups have suggested that apemen must leave the forests and head for the mountains, where they could live in holes in the rock.

Travel gives us creepers

OUR public transport system is in desperate need of a complete overhaul, claims a pressure group.

OfTree reckons that 90 per cent of tree creepers are smelly, noisy and packed with travellers.

And its survey showed long delays in rush hour journey times because of huge queues for creepers.

A spokesman for OfTree said: "The system is creaking. There's really not room to swing a chimp in most forests nowadays."

Transport groups have been advising apemen to try alternative travel systems, like crawling or rolling over and over.

Unfortunately, crawling hurts your knees and rolling makes you dizzy.

Inferno hell for apemen

REPORTS were coming in last night of a disaster involving an exploding mountain in Africa.

Apparently the mountain — or volcano as it is correctly termed — went berserk and started belching fire and this hot red liquid called lava from its top.

Many trees seem to have been burned to cinders in the inferno — making hundreds of families homeless.

An apeman who saw the blast said: "It was terrifying. I dug a hole and put my head in it until the noise stopped."

Another apeman is said to have died after he mistook a stream of lava for a river and drank some.

UPROAR AS TOFFS DEMAND RIGHT TO HUNT MAMMOTH

Pro-hunting . . . Mr Pith Frenzy

By CHUCK SPEAR, Political Editor

FURY erupted last night after an affluent group of apemen demanded the right to hunt down mammoths and kill them.

The apemen, many of whom live in large trees and are in charge of small communities, reckon the huge beasts could even be EATEN if we run out of berries and nuts.

Spokesman Pith Frenzy said the hunting of the mammoths is necessary because they are nasty large creatures which often frighten small children.

He said: "We think they are a potential danger. We plan to stalk them for days on end until they are exhausted then kill them with multiple stab wounds.

"Or we could goad them with sharp sticks until they run over a cliff and crash to their deaths below. It will be quite humane."

Fishy

But last night a newly-formed protest group named Friends of the Mammoth accused the pro-hunting apes of being savages who simply wanted to kill something for the fun of it.

Their spokesman Pith Pacifist said: "We're appalled by this bloodlust. These people don't realise what a kind and gentle creature the mammoth is. No one has been gored by one for weeks."

Mr Pacifist also poured scorn on the idea that we might one day eat dead mammoths.

He added: "It's a totally ludicrous suggestion. I suppose they think we'll soon be eating those funny fishy things, too?"

Friend or foe . . . some reckon mammoth is a gentle giant, but others say it is a woolly fiend

Anti-hunting . . . Mr Pith Pacifist

PITHS PUT TWO FEET IN IT

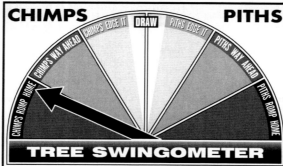

CHIMPS — PITHS

CHIMPS ROMP HOME | CHIMPS WAY AHEAD | CHIMPS EDGE IT | DRAW | PITHS EDGE IT | PITHS WAY AHEAD | PITHS ROMP HOME

TREE SWINGOMETER

THE Chimps had the 'Piths on the ropes as the tree-swinging row exploded into fury during Primate Minister's question time yesterday.

The Piths demanded to know whether there was any truth in leaked rumours that the Chimps were thinking of scrapping their long-held support of treetop living.

The Piths claimed a recent internal report by the Chimps showed that living nearer the ground IS safer, as the Piths maintain.

The Chimps hit back in devastating style.

They insisted they had NO concerns about living at altitude.

And to catcalls and great screeches of delight, they revealed that even certain influential Piths were now secretly doubting the wisdom of bipedalism and ground-living.

The humiliated Piths could only stumble off and lick their wounds.

PAGE TREE GIRL

Elegant 'Elm' is chimply the best

● OAK-AY lads, take a peep at a girl who's guaranteed to get the sap rising in any tree-dweller fella — our lovely Elm Acpherson.

As yew can see, the willowy brunette, 22, has looks that are beyond beleaf and a figure that makes her extremely poplar at parties.

● Sun readers have already gone ape for Elm, known as "The Trunk". They recently chose her as the girl they'd most like to spend time lying on a beech with. Later she was voted Primate of the Year by Playape mag.

● So if you're already pining for more glimpses of our beautiful babe-oon, don't go bananas. There is a host of pictures of Elm in next month's edition of Upright, the No1 magazine for red-blooded australopithecines.

● So make sure you rush out and order your copy now. You'll feel like a forest chump if you miss it.

UPRIGHT
The magazine for australopithecines
Fast & Lucy
INSIDE: Good Scratch Guide

Lads' mag . . . next month's issue of Upright

2,500,000 BC

MAN EATS MEAT

MANKIND is thought to have begun eating meat about 2.5million years ago. The early australopithecines are likely to have survived on the apes' staple diet of leaves, nuts and berries. Certainly, an analysis of their teeth seems to bear this out — they were blunt and flat, which would have been little use when chewing meat.

Evidence suggests, however, that the last australopithecus, Robustus, became a carnivore.

Scientists working in an Ethiopian desert recently discovered remains of an australopithecine and some

sharpened stone tools not far from the jaw of an antelope and bones of other animals. The remains date back 2.5million years, too early to be Homo Habilis, the first of the Homo species, though he was physically similar.

The animal bones had cut marks made by tools, showing the flesh had been stripped away.

The bones were broken at each end, showing that the australopithecine was trying to extract the marrow, a valuable new source of food. The desert area where the remains were found was once a shallow lake — indicating that the australopithecine was filleting the animals on the bank.

The possibility that Robustus was using tools is one of the many discrepancies in the study of early man. His successor was named Homo Habilis (Habilis meaning "handy man") specifically because he was originally thought to be the first to make tools. Some experts still hold this to be the case.

Homo Habilis emerged about 1.9million years ago, though it may have been as early as 2.4million years ago. His brain was significantly larger than the australopithecines' and it has been suggested that a meat-based, as opposed to plant-based, diet could have been responsible for this growth. It is also possible that his brain

expanded to cope with the extra thought processes required to make and use tools.

Homo Erectus, which evolved around 1.8million years ago, was the first hominid to leave Africa. He was making tools as advanced as cleavers — and hunting was in full swing.

Homo Erectus was a remarkably successful creature who learned to adapt to different environments, made tools, lived in caves and controlled fire. He is thought to have given rise both to Homo Sapiens Sapiens and to the Neanderthals, but survived in his own right, living alongside them, until as recently as 50,000 years ago.

Left, Homo Habilis making sharpened stole tools in order to butcher a carcass and, right, moving off in search of more prey, leaving the animal to vultures. Habilis and the last australopithecine are thought to have been the first hominids to eat meat

Family of Australopithecus Afarensis (see Lucy, Page 16). They walked upright but still climbed trees (3.5m)

..Timeline...

4m Australopithecus Afarensis appears (extinct 2.7m BC).

3.6m Date of fossilised footprints found in northern Tanzania which prove 'Piths walked on two feet.

3.5m Approximate date "Lucy" lived in Ethiopia. She is most famous Australopithecus Afarensis skeleton yet found.

3m Australopithecus Africanus appears (extinct by 2m BC) in Transvaal, South Africa.

Early tools, showing increasing sophistication as man developed — from pebble tool on left (about 2m) to hand-axes (1m and 350,000)

THE Sun

Thursday, May 28, 2497908BC

THOUGHT: FUTURE'S AT STEAK

'Shelters' to beat rain

By WALTER REPELLENT

AN amazing new contraption will stop you getting wet when it rains, its makers claimed last night.

The "shelter", made of leaves, branches or even an animal skin, can be put up between two trees and **DEFLECTS** water droplets as they fall.

The larger its surface area, the greater the number of people who can hide beneath it. The shelter, likely to be in production within a few thousand years, has huge advantages over the "cowering in a cave" system for avoiding showers, because it is portable.

There is even speculation that more sturdy shelters could provide us with permanent places to live.

Step-By-Step Guide — See Page 9

CHEW THE JURY

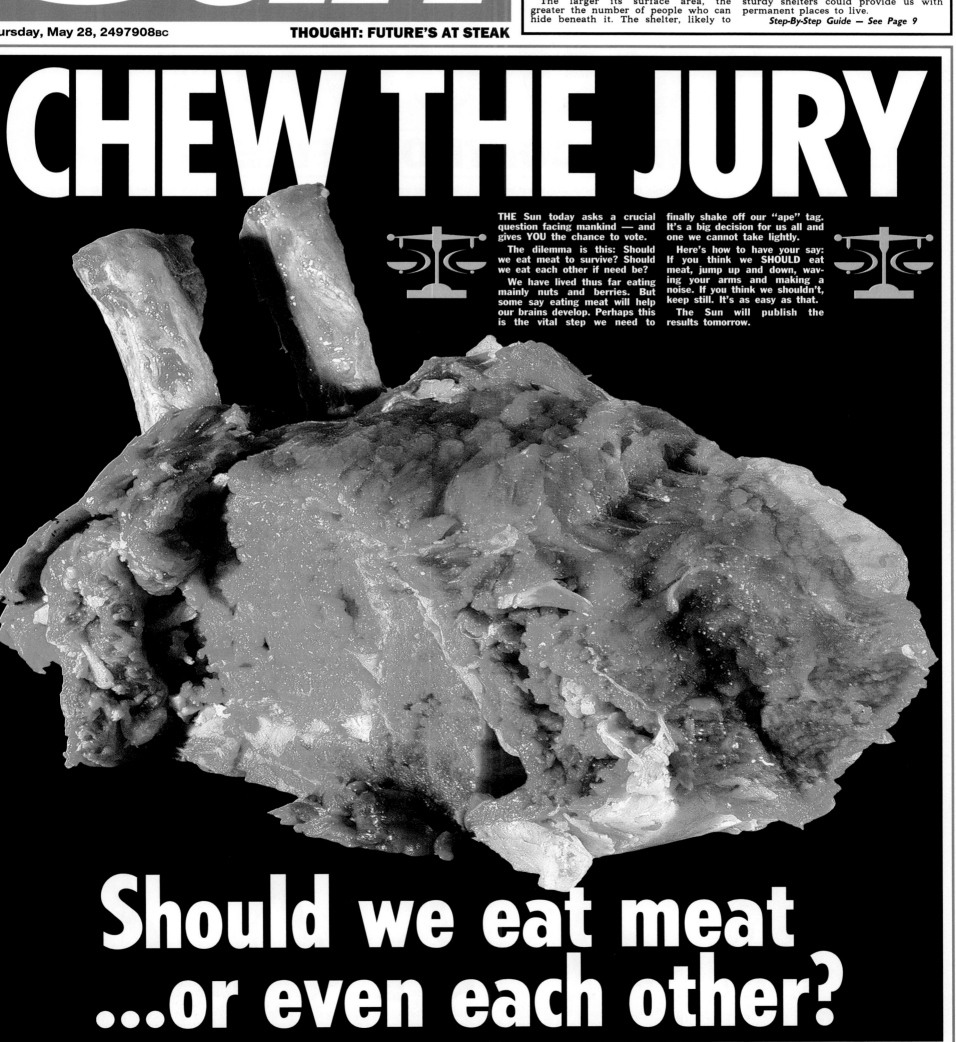

THE Sun today asks a crucial question facing mankind — and gives YOU the chance to vote.

The dilemma is this: Should we eat meat to survive? Should we eat each other if need be?

We have lived thus far eating mainly nuts and berries. But some say eating meat will help our brains develop. Perhaps this is the vital step we need to finally shake off our "ape" tag. It's a big decision for us all and one we cannot take lightly.

Here's how to have your say: If you think we SHOULD eat meat, jump up and down, waving your arms and making a noise. If you think we shouldn't, keep still. It's as easy as that.

The Sun will publish the results tomorrow.

Should we eat meat ...or even each other?

164,817,087 DAYS TO GO

450,000 BC

MAN CONTROLS FIRE

MASTERY of fire was a key breakthrough in mankind's development and set him on the road to civilisation.

It kept him warm in cold climates, allowing him to spread much further than before.

It offered him protection against predators and enabled him for the first time to cook.

There is plenty of dispute over when this development took place, but it seems likely not to have happened until around 450,000BC.

Humans long before that were, of course, no strangers to fire.

Lightning will often have sparked terrifying infernos — and the initial challenge was to control them. It is possible that this was achieved by Homo Erectus as early as 1.4million BC. Fossil sites in Africa which date back that far, and where burned animal bones have been discovered, seem to bear this out.

Controlling a fire started by nature is one thing, actually having the skill to start fire and use it is another — and this transition is thought to have taken hundreds of thousands of years.

The oldest hearths yet found, in Germany, Hungary and China, date back at the earliest to 450,000BC and possibly as late as 300,000BC.

It is not known exactly how early humans started their fires.

The two most likely methods are through creating sparks by striking a piece of flint against iron pyrites or by building up intense heat through friction by drilling into wood.

Once achieved, fire became an essential tool.

It enabled Homo Sapiens, who was physically adapted only for the tropics of Africa, to spread throughout Europe in around 200,000BC.

Though early humans were already using caves for shelter, fire would have made that much easier, providing heat and light.

Homo Sapiens, including the Neanderthals, learned to use fire in combat or to corner prey during a hunt. They used it to clear forests of brush so game could be seen more easily. Much later, with the advent of agriculture around 8,000BC, farmers used fire to clear fields and produce ash to act as fertiliser.

The ability to cook food was a great advantage — and one which had a direct effect on mankind's physical development.

In the harsh climate of Europe 300,000 years ago, game would often freeze after being killed and thus cooking became essential, if only to thaw food out.

Cooked meat, of course, needs far less cutting and gnawing than raw meat — and gradually mankind's need for large teeth to rip and endlessly chew flesh became less and less. One of the significant physical differences between Homo Erectus and Homo Sapiens is that the latter has much smaller jaws and teeth.

...Timeline...

2.2m Rough date for first emergence, in Africa, of the first Homo, Homo Habilis — makes primitive tools and shelters. Like Australopithecus Robustus, he eats meat.

1.9m The more advanced Homo Erectus migrates from southern Africa into the north of the continent — he has bigger brain, uses axes and cleavers, lives in caves and simple houses.

1.8m Beginning of the Cenozoic Era's Quaternary Period (Pleistocene Epoch).

1.5m Homo Habilis extinct; The long Ice Age begins.

1.4m Possible date at which mankind learns to control fires started by nature — he would not start one himself for the best part of a million years.

1m Homo Erectus migrates out of Africa — he is able to colonise Europe and Asia, possibly through his ability to live in self-supporting social groups.

600000 The Homo Erectus line begins to diverge into two strands, eventually recognisable as Homo Sapiens Sapiens and the Neanderthals.

500000 Beginning of Cenozoic Era, Quaternary Period's Lower Palaeolithic age, also known as Old Stone Age; Date of Britain's earliest human remains, "Boxgrove Man", unearthed in gravel pit at Boxgrove, Sussex.

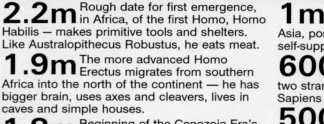

Scene from 450,000 BC based on so-called Peking Man discoveries in a cave at Zhoukudian near Beijing. Skulls of Homo Erectus, including the one shown left, were found with tools and charcoal remains of a fire

Various stages in our development, from small ape Aegyptopithecus to the larger Proconsul, which may have spawned Australopithecus (not shown), then the similar-looking but more advanced Homo Habilis, then Homo Erectus. Neanderthals (5th from left) did evolve from Erectus but are not direct ancestors of Homo Sapiens Sapiens (far right)

THE Sun

Friday, August 19, 451554BC

THOUGHT: NOW WE'RE COOKING

FLAME AT LAST

Man figures out how to start fire

A MAN successfully started a fire for the first time last night.

The historic break-through was achieved in Germany using flint to generate sparks.

It has enormous implica-

By BERNIE FLINT

tions for the future of the world. We learned many years ago to control fires started by lightning and even to use it for our own ends.

But being able to start fires will allow us to keep warm in even the coldest climates,

where so far we have been unable to spread.

It will also give us more opportunities to cook our food, which will be kinder to our teeth as it cuts down the gnawing required.

● Now **YOU** can start a fire — see our cut-out-and-keep instructions: Centre Pages

ARE YOU A BRIGHT SPARK?

MANKIND'S evolution is hotting up, folks! But there's so much MORE we need. So today The Sun asks YOU to think up ideas to transform the human race. Some way of fighting off disease, per-

haps, or some method of communicating with each other. Maybe some way of avoiding having to WALK everywhere. Send us your ideas. We'll pay an animal carcass for each one we publish.

36,171,836 DAYS TO GO

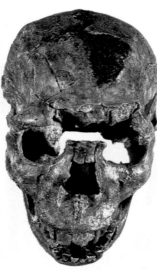

Left, the skull and bones of a neanderthal man found in a cave in France in 1908. Top, the skull of a Homo Erectus. While this example is 1.6m years old, Homo Erectus still existed during this period and even later (see 300000)

100,000 BC

MANKIND TALKS

LIFE as we know it would be impossible without language — and yet it is a remarkably recent development in our evolution. It is pure speculation to try to place a date on when this change took place — but it seems nonetheless true that only we — Homo Sapiens Sapiens — have had the physical attributes capable of producing sounds varied enough to convey meaningful amounts of information.

It is probable that language, above all else, allowed modern humans to flourish while others like the Neanderthals died out.

All mammals produce sounds by expelling air from the lungs through the vocal cords in the larynx, or Adam's Apple. The difference in modern humans is that our larynx is low in the throat compared with other animals, giving us a large resonating cavity above it through which we filter sound. This enables us, by varying the positions of the tongue and lips, to produce a wide range of sounds of which animals are incapable.

Scientists used fossil evidence to recreate the vocal tract of a Neanderthal Man who co-existed in Europe with Homo Sapiens Sapiens during the Ice Age. They found that because of his relatively high larynx and flat tongue he would have been incapable even of producing our basic vowel sounds. The modern humans living in Europe at the time (the so-called Cro-Magnon Man) had a vocal tract capable of producing all the sounds we use today. They survived, the Neanderthals did not.

There is no evidence as to exactly how language first evolved, though it is likely it began as a series of grunted vowel sounds and that consonants came as man developed more control over manipulating his tongue, teeth and lips.

Eventually the brain evolved and grew larger to cope with storing vocabulary, interpreting many different sounds and arranging words in different orders to mean different things. This is now part of our genetic make-up — children inherit the ability to learn language.

The brain also learned to control speech and to stay silent when necessary. This is something we take for granted, but chimps, for example, have almost no control over the noises they make to express emotion and are almost incapable of suppressing them even when they know they will alert a predator.

Language gave our Cro-Magnon predecessors many advantages over their competitors, such as the ability to warn others in their social group of danger, tell them the location of food or water, plan for the future and learn from the experiences of previous generations.

It enabled them to create a culture based around their history and mythology. And it gave them the ability to deceive and manipulate.

...Timeline...

300000 Date of the earliest known Neanderthal remains — he has evolved from Homo Erectus, though Erectus is not extinct.

250000 Beginning of Cenozoic Era, Quarternary Period's Middle Palaeolithic age; Date of the oldest known "art" — a small figure carved from volcanic rock, found at Berekhat Ram, Israel.

200000 The First appearance of Homo Sapiens Sapiens,

who, like the Neanderthals, has evolved from Homo Erectus. He is brighter and more resourceful than the Neanderthals and able to hunt more efficiently. Homo Sapiens is still in Africa, though, while the Neanderthals have spread further afield.

135000 The Neanderthals now dominate Europe and Western Asia — they are heavily-built, live in settlements, make tools and bury their dead.

Left, model of a neanderthal group during a burial ceremony in a cave (see 135000). Right, a hunting scene featuring early Homo Sapiens using spears as they chase a fleeing deer 250,000 years ago on the banks of a river in Britain

THE Sun

Thursday, December 1, 99101BC

THOUGHT: IT'S YOUR SHOUT

UG

Man's first word agreed in historic vote by cavemen

THE first word of mankind's first language was formally agreed last night. It is to be "Ug".

The simple but effective monosyllable topped a list of contenders which included "Eh", "Ah" and "Ooh".

It was praised by its caveman judges for its capacity to be used for a variety of purposes, for conveying a sense of urgency and for being pronounceable by just about everybody.

"Ug" will specifically denote anything that the speaker is pointing at.

It is thought that men, in particular, will be able to get by with just this one word for many centuries and possibly millennia.

However, while it is accepted that Ug is a fine starting-point, it is

By GABBY LOT and ELLIE CUTION

thought that other words may in due course be necessary.

These will mainly need to be vowel-based until such time as mankind learns to co-ordinate his throat, tongue and lips to produce a variety of consonants.

MOCK

One of the key advantages in Homo Sapiens Sapiens developing language is that it will enable him to mock the Neanderthals, whose larynx and tongue are not built for speaking.

More seriously, it could also enable him to dominate the Neanderthals.

Simple sentences like "I know where there is food" will be understandable by Homo Sapiens Sapiens, but not by any other species.

PETER PIPER PICKS PECK OF PICKLED PEPPER - Pages 4 & 5

COUNTDOWN TO CHRIST

28,973,290 DAYS TO GO

80,000 BC

THE ICE AGE

Arctic snow and ice in the sunset. For many thousands of years, from about 80000BC, this is how enormous areas of northern Europe, North America and Asia looked. As cold summers failed to thaw winter ice, a great glacier gradually spread south from the Arctic. In places it was two miles high. Life must have been very hard indeed

IT is a remarkable testament to mankind's ability to adapt to different and challenging environments that he survived the Ice Age. Between 80,000BC and around 7,000BC the world's average temperature fell by about 15 degrees centigrade, leaving almost a quarter of the Earth's current land mass under ice. Man had to adapt fast — and did so.

But this was only one of many Ice Ages to have gripped the Earth over its 4.6billion-year history.

In fact, what we call the Ice Age is really only a particularly cold "blip" in a major Ice Age which began 1.6million years ago and is still going on. During this long period, the Pleistocene Epoch, the Earth has had about 20 such "glaciations", followed by warmer interglacial periods during which it is relatively warm — warmer, in fact, than it is now.

From about 80,000BC ice from the Arctic spread south until it covered vast swathes of northern Europe, Asia and America under glaciers hundreds of feet thick. In some places it is thought to have been TWO MILES thick.

The only respite for the people of those times was that the winters did not become much more bitter, it was simply that summers became colder, giving the winter ice no chance to melt. The following winter's ice added to that of the previous year and never thawed.

Over thousands of years the ice would have grown into a huge wall, beyond which people could not venture.

Had anyone been able to climb it and stand at the top, they would have encountered a vast sheet of ice stretching as far as the eye could see.

Many animal species were destroyed by the cold. Camels, llamas and horses, all native to America, were driven out.

It was thousands of years before man reintroduced horses there.

Other animals fared better — reindeer, mammoths, bears and wolves. Despite the conditions our direct ancestors, the early Homo Sapiens Sapiens, emerged from Africa and spread northwards. By this time they had great advantages — language, mastery of fire, clothing and a range of bone, antler and stone tools.

They made good use of caves to shelter from the cold — and left art and artefacts there.

The Neanderthals, with their strong, compact bodies ideally suited for a cold climate, lived alongside these modern humans for thousands of years.

But by the time the ice began to melt, Homo Sapiens Sapiens was the only hominid left.

...Timeline...

A family preparing a meal in their cave during the Ice Age. Caves provided excellent shelter from the harsh climate

80000 Start of Ice Age, an extra-cold "blip" in the longer-term ice age which began 1.6million years ago and which is still going on. Vast quantities of water freeze at poles, lowering sea levels and the resulting land bridges link most of the world's land mass into one huge continent. This allows Homo Sapiens Sapiens to spread from Africa throughout most of the world. At this point he is co-existing with Neanderthals — and probably Homo Erectus too — in Europe and the Near East.

Neanderthals were well suited to the cold. Here, they are seen attacking a bear, an animal which thrived during the Ice Age

BANK HOLIDAY Sun

Monday, February 14, 79379BC

THOUGHT: ZERO TOLERANCE

PHEW What a scorcher

It shore looks tempting . . . beach yesterday as heat soared to zero

Temperature hits 0° C

IT'S another Bank Holiday sizzler, folks — today's temperature is set to rocket to 0°C!

So grab the kids, get out of the cave and bask in the balmy Arctic breeze.

Last night families were already flocking to the shores in

By IVOR SCARFE

their skimpiest summer furs. For the children there were stone tools for making ice castles. For the dads, sharpened sticks for warding off bears.

Weathermen say the frozen spell will last 70,000 years — and then it'll get even **WARMER**.

Balmy Army — Page 5

IT'S THAT FURSACE OUTFIT AGAIN

★ TASTY Tracey Troglodyte shows off her mammoth assets — as she turns up for a party wearing her famous Fursace outfit.

The sexy huntress caused a stir as she arrived at last night's premiere of the new cave painting Slaughtered Bison. One man in the crowd said: "She looks good enough to eat — and actually that's not a bad idea."

★ Tracey, 23, first unveiled the revealing wolf skin number at a bear-skinning festival last year. She was later voted the woman men would most like to drag around their cave by the hair.

WHITE NEAN MAN

A view of Britain
from inside the cave

TODAY'S White Nean Man, who calls himself Aaargh Aaaaargh, is 27 and lives in the second cave on the right, near the big glacier.

Aaargh, a Neanderthal father of 17 who communicated with Sun man IAN COMPREHENSIBLE using grunts and sign language, discusses the burning issues of the day.

WEATHER experts reckon that we're heading for a hot spell, with temperatures soaring to freezing point.

WNM: About time, I'd say. It'll make a nice change to be able to put the winter clothes away. I've had this deerskin jacket on for the past 16 years.

On the subject of clothes, women's fashions are getting skimpier and skimpier.

WNM: It's nice to see the ladies showing off a bit of flesh. But I've warned my missus not to get carried away — frostbite can be nasty. She always makes sure she coats her exposed parts with wild boar fat. It gives her quite a sexy aroma!

Homo Sapiens is flooding into this part of Europe from Africa.

WNM: I don't have a problem with them, to be honest. I mean they're so thin and sickly-looking I can't seem them thriving here. I reckon that the first real cold snap will wipe them all out.

Cave prices have been rising steadily for the past 1.4million years — but experts predict they could rocket by as much as 200 per cent in the next few months because of a shortage.

WNM: The cost of caves now is ridiculous. The missus and I looked at a new cave recently — one room, fireplace, the usual bison-hunting scene on the wall. They wanted four funny-shaped stones for it! I just laughed. I later heard that a bloke from the other side of the glacier was about to offer the asking price, but was gazumped by a Homo Sapiens who paid two antelope skulls and a pointy stick!

The warmer weather is increasing the birth-rate among animals like deer and bears.

WNM: This should mean there'll be more meat available, which is a relief. Last year we were so desperate we had to eat one of the neighbour's kids. And it was tough.

A new report claims that speaking is gaining in popularity — with new words being invented every day.

WNM: It makes me laugh, this speaking lark. What's the use of it? I had a row with one of these speakers the other day over which of us had killed this bear. He started yelling this strange gibberish and waving his arms. I simply raised my spear and stabbed him in the eye. Not a word was uttered, but I think I got my point across!

A recent study suggested obesity is becoming a big problem among neanderthals — with the majority of males weighing more than 12st, even though they are not much over 5ft in height.

WNM: I think this is just a fad. I like to tuck into a couple of small mammals a day. Well, you can't just get by on nuts and berries, can you? Most of us are not fat, we've just got big bones. I mean, my eyebrows alone must weigh more than half a stone.

Neanderthal numbers are said to be dwindling — sparking fears that the species may become extinct in the not too distant furture.

WNM: You can tell we're in the silly season when the "Neanderthals Face Destruction" stories are wheeled out. They've been predicting our doom for millennia, and we're still going strong.

SO SEXY IT'S
SKINFUL

BEACHWEAR

Sun FASHION SPECIAL

IT'S time to chuck away those bearskins, girls — because the latest sexy fashion is going to be all about BARE skin!

So if you don't want to look like an endangered species, throw off those ankle-length furs and flash that flesh.

The key word in the coming millennium is going to be skimpy — with all the top designers chopping away the fabric to flaunt luscious legs, muscular midriffs and tantalising torsos. Even the boys will

By TANYA HIDE, Fashion Editor

be flinging back the covers to let us peek at their perfect pecs.

Here, we give you a glimpse of some of the slinky skins that we'll soon be wearing whether we're bathing at the beach (left), hunting with the lads, hobnobbing with pals at a barbecue or joining in a frenzied religious rite.

Pictures by NEAL LITHICK

HUNTING CHIC
Lads look dead sexy as they slaughter a huge mammoth

DINNER DATE *Fur-lined deerskin trousers worn with a plunging neckline look great at barbecue*

SUNDAY BEST *A classy outfit for any animal sacrifice ritual. And those ugly bloodstains wash out easily*

30,000 BC

DEATH OF NEANDERTHALS

NEANDERTHAL Man is traditionally seen as a sluggish, lumpen, moronic brute — and yet he was nothing of the kind. The prejudice dates back to early last century when scientists wrongly reconstructed a Neanderthal skeleton to show it slouching along with its knees bent.

In fact, Neanderthal Man walked fully upright.

His brain was bigger than ours and he showed cultural sophistication far in advance of his traditional image.

That said, he died out around 30,000 years ago, probably because he was unable to compete with the more adaptable and skilled Homo Sapiens Sapiens with whom he shared the planet for many thousands of years.

Neanderthals were named after the Neander Valley in Germany ("thal" is German for valley), where their fossils were first found in 1856.

A genetic test carried out on those fossils in 1997 seems to prove that modern man is NOT descended from the neanderthals — because their DNA differs fundamentally from ours.

It is now thought that some 600,000 years ago the descendants of Homo Erectus began gradually to split into two different species, the neanderthals and the ancestors of modern humans.

Neanderthals are among the most well-studied of the early humans, partly because they lived relatively recently and also because they habitually lived in limestone caves, which preserve bones well.

The earliest known neanderthal dates back about 300,000 years, some 100,000 before the first modern humans. They lived over a widespread area from western Europe to central Asia and, compared with their predecessors, were highly advanced.

They were the first humans to bury their dead. Artefacts found in the graves have led to speculation that they had a religion and believed in the afterlife, though this is hotly debated.

Neanderthals made comparatively sophisticated stone tools and spears and could make fire. They adorned themselves with simple pendants.

Short, stocky and immensely strong, they were perfectly built to conserve heat in the harsh conditions of the Ice Age. Males averaged 5ft 5ins but weighed 185lb. Females averaged 5ft and weighed 176lb. They had low foreheads, large noses, jutting brows and a bony arch over each eye.

Their skeletons were heavier than those of modern humans. Their shoulders were broad, their chests large and their arms, legs, hands and feet extremely powerful.

Around 80,000BC, modern humans emerged from Africa and over the next 50,000 years spread north into the Middle East, Asia and Europe where the neanderthals lived.

More resourceful than the neanderthals, they were more able to adapt to different climates and thus to spread further afield. They hunted and gathered food more efficiently and formed larger social groups.

There is no evidence that they actively hunted neanderthals to extinction. Study of neanderthal behaviour seems to point to a species simply unable to cope with the competition.

Planning and thought was not their strong point.

They lived in small groups, successfully hunting small animals and scavenging from the carcasses of larger ones, but it seems to have been an entirely opportunistic process without the systems used by the modern humans.

And while they could make and control fire, their hearths were too shallow to sustain it to keep them warm throughout a night.

As a result a neanderthal's life was harsh. All adult skeletons have signs of serious injury. The majority have evidence of malnutrition. Average life expectancy was under 40.

Perhaps the modern humans' greatest advantage over the neanderthals was the power of speech.

It seems to be the case that language — enabling humans to plan ahead, warn others of danger and form complex social groups and relationships — developed only in the last 100,000 years.

It may well be that the neanderthals were simply incapable of it.

Left, a neanderthal. Above, a cave-dwelling neanderthal family watch out warily for Homo Sapiens aggressors. There is no evidence, though, that the two species fought

...Timeline...

71000 Eruption of Sumatra's Toba volcano covers parts of India in 10ft of ash and further lowers worldwide temperature for 1,000 years.

60000 Beginning of Cenozoic Era's Upper Palaeolithic age.

50000 Cro-Magnon Man (the name for European Homo Sapiens during the Ice Age) uses baskets and carefully-crafted weapons — his complex social groups allow him to adapt to different climates and conditions; Australia is reached for the first time; Homo Erectus dies out after nearly two million years.

45000 Date of a neanderthal carving found on woolly mammoth tooth near Tata, Hungary.

40000 First encampment using tents, in Moldova, south-east Europe; Japan is colonised, so is New Guinea.

30000 Neanderthals die out — unable to compete with, or spread as successfully as, Homo Sapiens Sapiens; Date of oldest known animal carving, an ivory horse discovered near Vogelherd, Germany.

This species is no more.. it has ceased to be.. this is an EX species

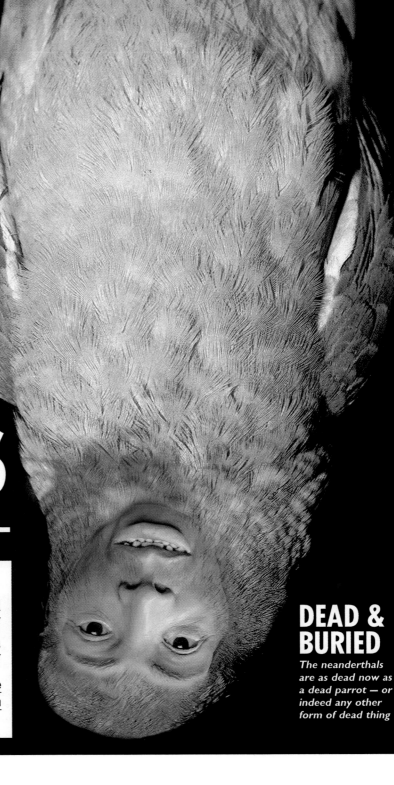

DEAD & BURIED

The neanderthals are as dead now as a dead parrot — or indeed any other form of dead thing

---

THE Sun takes no pleasure today in announcing the demise of the neanderthals.

It is, in fact, a sad duty to report that as of last night they are as dead as, well . . . a dead parrot.

For hundreds of thousands of years this once-proud species stood for all that was good about mankind.

Their views reflected **OUR** views — particularly on the importance of food and shelter. But if we learn one thing from the neanderthals it is this — you

PAGE ONE OPINION

must change with the times. It's all very well developing short, stocky bodies to conserve heat in an Ice Age.

But you won't get far unless you speak the people's language — or any language for that matter.

The world must pick itself up and move on. The best man won — and the best man was Cro-Magnon Man.

7,020,519 DAYS TO GO

20,000 BC

CAVE PAINTINGS AND EARLY ART

IT is hard for us to imagine men and women tens or even hundreds of thousands of years ago having the sensitivity to create works of art. But they did. In fact, from about 30,000BC there was an explosion in art around the world, taking two forms — cave paintings and small carved objects.

There are artefacts from far earlier which could be considered art. The oldest known such object, a piece of volcanic rock found at Berekhat Ram, Israel, dates from 250,000 years ago and is thought to be a carving of the female form.

Other objects dating from 200,000BC to 50,000BC have been found in Europe and are simple pendants made from tooth and bone, probably by neanderthals. Various kinds of

symbolic objects were made between 50,000BC and 30,000BC, but it is then that prehistoric art truly took off.

The peoples of that time, particularly the Cro-Magnons who inhabited Europe, took to wearing intricate jewellery made of stone, ivory, antler and bone. They carved figurines of humans and animals and sculpted images of the female body with exaggerated breasts and hips, possibly as fertility symbols. These have become known as Venus figures.

More spectacular are the extraordinary cave paintings, found mainly in northern Spain and southern France. Some of the most famous — the paintings of various animals at Altamira, Spain — were treated with suspicion by archaeologists when first

discovered in 1880. But others were then found, and prehistoric cave paintings were officially recognised by 1902. New finds are still being made. The oldest known cave paintings, dating back 32,000 years, were found in the Ardeche Valley in south-east France as recently as 1995.

Cave paintings are generally of horses, bison, deer and mammoths and occasionally birds and fish. They were done with red pigment (iron oxide found in clay) and black pigment (manganese or charcoal), probably using fingers or sticks or even simple animal-hair brushes.

Hand stencils, like the one on the page opposite, involved the artists blowing paint on to the wall directly from their mouths or a tube of some

kind. The meaning behind the Cro-Magnon cave paintings is unknown. They may have been purely for enjoyment and decoration. But it is intriguing that so few different animal species were ever depicted, that so much cave art appears in inaccessible places and that some of it was done in caves that were not lived in.

Researchers have found that the most richly-decorated caves are those with the best acoustics, lending weight to the notion that the paintings were linked to some kind of ceremony.

Some scientists believe they were part of a ritual designed to ensure a successful hunt, others that they were done as a symbolic encouragement to animals to propagate and provide humans with more food.

Cave paintings and rock art continued for many thousands of years. These figures in Colorado, U.S., are probably as recent as 1000BC

Cow and ponies from spectacular cave at Lascaux, Montignac, France (30000BC). The art there is some of the most beautiful in the world

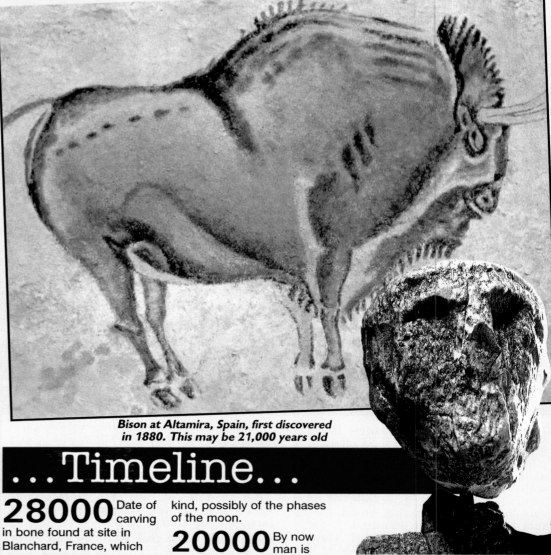

Bison at Altamira, Spain, first discovered in 1880. This may be 21,000 years old

A man carved from mammoth bone, found in Czechoslovakia (38000BC)

...Timeline...

28000 Date of carving in bone found at site in Blanchard, France, which shows Cro-Magnon man was making notes of some kind, possibly of the phases of the moon.

20000 By now man is creating intricate cave paintings and has a religion.

THE Sun

Tuesday, April 2, 19235BC   **THOUGHT: PRINTS OF DARKNESS**

MEET THE ICE GIRLS See Pages 16 & 17

Makeover team wrecked my cave

Trendy . . . floppy-haired makeover chief

Disgruntled . . . angry caveman Ug last night

FURIOUS Ug Grunter told last night how a trendy "makeover" team decorated his cave — and WRECKED it.

Ug invited them to paint a prancing buffalo to add some vitality to his lounge.

But after a day out hunting and gathering, he returned to find a garish

By TATE MODERN

"handprint stencil" all over the main wall. Ug, 35, of Ardeche, France, said last: "They seem simply to have got a load of pigment in their mouths and **SPAT** it over their hands. I don't think I'll ever be able to get it off."

A spokesman for the team said: "We're always doing bisons and stuff — we thought we'd try something else."

THEY WASHED THEIR HANDS IN MY BISON - Page 7

Deidre's photo cavebook

ROCKY'S NAGGING MISSUS: DAY 1

Rocky's mates invite him to come on a weekend stag hunting extravaganza

But Rocky's wife bans him from going because she wants the cave painted

Sad Rocky imagines his pals having fun as he daubs a bison

Rocky's mates return — and taunt him for being under his wife's thumb

Deidre says Perhaps you simply need to explain to your wife that slaughtering defenceless animals with your mates is just your way of letting off steam. I'm sure she'll realise she's being a bit unreasonable. If this doesn't work, try clubbing her repeatedly around the head. I'm sending you my leaflet Beating Your Partner Into Submission.

ICE TO SEE YOU TO SEE YOU ICE

By PHIL SPACE, Showbiz Editor

★ TODAY Sun readers can chill out with the biggest pop sensation since the Big Bang — the Ice Girls.

★ Fans say the fab four are cooler than any glaciers — and have made more impact than the asteroid that wiped out the dinosaurs millions of years back.

★ The girls, Spotty Ice, Rabid Ice, Scarry Ice and Wash Ice, have already built up a huge following thanks to their smash hits like Wannafreeze, 2 Become Warm and Mamath.

★ Yesterday the girls came into The Sun's HQ to pose for these super igloosive pictures.

★ And below we give an in-depth profile of each of the girls — so you can find out just what makes them such hot stuff.

SPOTTY

FUN-loving tomboy Spotty, 18, is definitely the tearaway of the group.

She gets her name from the trademark red blotches that cover her entire body — the only remaining signs of a virulent plague that wiped out more than two thirds of her tribe when she was a baby.

Spotty says: "I love animals, especially bears. My ambition is to hunt one down and skin it."

SCARRY

SEXY Scarry just loves dressing up and is always in trouble for borrowing the other girls' furs.

The evil-looking gashes that cover most of her face gave her the name Scarry.

The 21-year-old explains: "The scars come from an amusing encounter I had with a sabre-toothed tiger four years ago. I can laugh now but it was scary at the time — the tiger ate three of my sisters!"

RABID

BLONDE bombshell Rabid is the baby of the band at just 17.

She was raised by a pack of wild dogs as a tot — and still loves to be patted on the head by the other girls.

And that's not her only canine trick . . . when she gets excited she howls and foams at the mouth — giving rise to the nickname Rabid! She said: "I often howl on stage. The fans love it."

WASH

SQUEAKY-clean Wash gets her name from a bizarre habit — she likes to cover herself with water and scrub off the layers of grime!

Wash, 21, said: "I know it's a strange thing to do, but I really enjoy it."

The Sun's childcare expert AUNTY BIOTIC says: "Young girls should NOT copy Wash. The layers of grime are there to protect your body and should never be removed."

2,380,067 DAYS TO GO

Joshua attacks Jericho (founded 8350). The Bible says the Israelite leader took the city by marching round it — a trumpet blast then brought the walls tumbling down

...Timeline...

16000 Half of modern-day Britain is covered in ice, in places hundreds of metres thick.

15000 Man reaches the Americas from Siberia — continent is teeming with wildlife including three types of mammoth, camels, giant bison, giant beavers and giant cats. They are hunted so relentlessly they are all extinct on the continent within 5,000 years — including the horse, only re-introduced there from Europe in the 16th Century AD.

12000 The dog is domesticated.

11000 Deer and elk increase in Britain as climate gets warmer — grasslands and forests spring up from southern England to northern Scotland; Flint-edged wooden tools are used to gather wild grain.

10000 Temperatures rise as Ice Age draws to close — sea levels begin to rise, cutting off many regions and slowing migration. Peoples in each area begin to develop different cultures. By now there are about ten million people worldwide, surviving by hunting and gathering; Beginning of Cenozoic Era's Holocene Epoch; Date of an engraved antler found at Montgaudier, France, which shows a seal, salmon and plants; Metallurgy is practised in Anatolia (now Turkey).

9000 People of modern-day Iraq develop farming, a turning-point for mankind, allowing settlements to flourish by living off the land.

8350 World's first walled city, Jericho, is founded (in modern-day Israel) — covers ten acres.

8000 Large groups of hunters live at lakeside sites in Humberside region; Beginning of the Middle Stone Age (Mesolithic); The peoples of the Near and Middle East (present-day Syria, Iran, Iraq, Turkey, Jordan, Israel), cultivate lentils, peas and chick-peas.

7500 Date of earliest canoe paddle, in Yorkshire.

7000 First farming in Greece and Aegean; First use of copper, in Anatolia.

6500 Britain's 'land bridge' with continental Europe disappears around this time and the Ice Age is over.

A mud brick from Jericho, the world's first walled city (8350)

A mammoth skeleton found in Siberia. Scientists aim to clone one from DNA

6500 BC

THE ICE MELTS

Man probably hunted mammoths to extinction after walking into America across an Ice Age land bridge from Siberia. The thaw cut America off, as it did Britain (6500)

BRITAIN has only been an island for about 6,500 years. When the glaciation which we call the Ice Age began 80,000 years ago sea levels fell dramatically, as much as 500ft lower than they are today, because so much of our oceans was frozen at the poles.

The effect of this was to expose large tracts of land which had previously been under water.

Most of the major land masses of the world were thus linked.

Britain was joined to what is now France in the east and south, to Ireland in the west and to Scandinavia in the north-east.

Theoretically it would have been possible to walk from Britain, right across Scandinavia and Russia to Alaska and the rest of North America.

Indeed, the fact that most of the world was one enormous continent DID allow mankind to colonise huge areas of the Earth he had hitherto been unable to reach.

By 50,000BC men had reached Australia by boat thanks to the sea crossing being shorter than before. Japan was reached by 40,000BC across a land bridge from Korea exposed by the lower sea levels.

Around the same time North America was reached, probably because man was able to walk across what is now the Bering Strait — the channel between Alaska and Russia. As the ice began to melt, around 10,000BC, sea levels rose again and areas like America and Britain were cut off. In isolation, their people's culture and development began to evolve in different ways.

Scientists are unsure why ice ages happen.

Perhaps the most plausible theory is that put forward in the 1920s by Yugoslav scientist Milutin Milankovitch.

The Milankovitch Astronomical Theory says that ice ages are caused by a slight but regular deviation in the Earth's almost circular orbit around the sun.

This happens every 93,408 years and causes the Arctic to have particularly cold summers for up to a few thousand years — thus allowing an increase in glaciation.

Some scientists believe we are already heading for another ice age.

They say that a new glaciation generally begins within 10,000 to 20,000 years of the peak of the previous one.

It has been 18,000 years since the accepted peak of the last ice age — and evidence suggests that the world's average temperature HAD been falling for a few thousand years until two centuries ago when mankind's industrial revolution began the process of global warming.

THE Sun

Saturday, October 11, 6521BC

THOUGHT: THAW POINT

IT'S THE SUN WOT DUN IT

BRITAIN'S new-found independence from the continent is all thanks to the sun.

The Earth's orbit round the enormous, glowing ball of fire deviates every 90,000-odd years, causing the Arctic to get cold summers.

This means there's never enough warmth to melt the previous winter's ice — and an Ice Age sets in.

All that ice at the Poles is frozen sea water, so the sea level falls around the world and all the low-lying land is exposed. It was that which linked our country to everyone else's.

But now the Earth is back on track — and our No1 sun has melted vast quantities of ice at the Poles and all over the Northern Hemisphere.

So now we have glorious amounts of ocean to make us an island. Last night a spokesman for The Sun said: "Thank you, our sun."

Isle be seeing you

AN ISLAND AT LAST AS ICE MELTS

BRITAIN is an island at last, The Sun can announce today.

The melting of ice has caused a "channel" of water to cover low-lying areas in the east, cutting us off from the vast continent we used to be joined to.

And we can also gleefully reveal that the channel is getting **WIDER**.

Yesterday a family of Sun readers

By IAN DEPENDENCE

rushed to the coast to wave a cheery farewell to the continent.

It is the first time Britain has been isolated since before the Ice Age began about 75,000 years ago.

The enormous amounts of ice that built up began to melt about 3,500 years ago — and the Ice Age is now almost officially over.

Great Sun ferry offer — see Page 10

Great Sun ferry offer — see Page 10

PAGE ONE OPINION

FEELS good, doesn't it?

No one in our lifetime has been able to imagine the pride that being an island brings, until now. And while we wish our continental neighbours the best of luck with their futures . . .

We're delighted they'll never have a say over ours.

5500 BC
NOAH AND THE FLOOD

THE story of Noah and the great flood is one of the Old Testament's most famous episodes. New scientific evidence points to it being based on an immense Black Sea flood of around 5,500BC, caused by Ice Age glaciers melting. It was so catastrophic it was passed down through hundreds of generations by word of mouth.

Noah's life story is told in the book of Genesis, Chapters 5 to 9. According to Chapter 5, Noah — a tenth-generation descendant of Adam — was 500 years old when he fathered his three sons Shem, Ham and Japeth.

God was furious at mankind's violence and corruption and decided to wipe out all life with a flood. He liked Noah, however, and decided to spare him, his wife and sons and their wives.

God warned Noah about the impending 40-day-and-night flood and instructed him to build an enormous ship known as an ark. Noah was told to take his family with him on board, plus mating pairs of every kind of bird and animal. God provided detailed instructions on how to build the boat — it needed to be wooden, 450ft long, 75ft wide and 45ft deep, with three decks, a door in the side and a roof. Noah's family needed enough food for the duration of the flood. Noah followed the instructions to the letter.

Mythology says that unicorns were too flighty to slum it with other animals, so they refused their place on the ark . . . and perished.

Genesis says rain began falling on the 17th day of the second month in Noah's 600th year and fell for 40 days and nights. The water rose to cover the mountains and wiped out every living creature, but the ark remained afloat with its passengers intact.

Finally the rain stopped and the waters, over several months, subsided. As they did so, the ark was washed up on Mount Ararat.

Noah repeatedly sent out birds from the ark but they flew back because there was nowhere but water for them to land. Finally a dove returned with an olive leaf in its beak and Noah knew the waters had subsided enough for the bird to land in a tree branch.

By the first day of the first month of Noah's 601st year, the Earth had dried out. The ark's inhabitants disembarked and went off to multiply all over the world. God swore to Noah he would never inflict such a disaster on mankind again. He created rainbows which would appear to remind men of this promise. He also gave Noah and his descendants permission to eat meat.

Noah began farming, planted a vineyard, got drunk and crashed out naked in his tent, Genesis says. He lived another 350 years and died aged 950. The story leaves Noah as the father of all humanity, since all men except his sons died in the flood.

Genesis is not the only ancient work to describe a catastrophic flood, though. In fact, it is likely that the Noah story is based on an older account from ancient Mesopotamia.

In that version, a man called Utnapishtim is warned of a flood by the god Ea and told to build a ship for his family, servants and animals. After a week-long flood, the ship comes to rest on a mountain-top. The gods' anger is abated and Utnapishtim and his wife granted immortality. Similar legends are found in the Middle East.

The stories may all be based on the spectacular flood in 5,500BC. The Mediterranean burst through the Bosphorus Valley with incredible force, probably killing thousands of people and billions of animals on land and sea.

It has been calculated that it flowed for two years with the force of 200 Niagara Falls and a roar heard 300 miles away. It swamped the Black Sea, then a freshwater lake, and turned it overnight into a saltwater sea.

This theory was seemingly confirmed in 1998 when scientists found the remains of freshwater molluscs dating to 5,600BC some 550ft below the Black Sea's surface, followed by saltwater ones from 4,900BC. They also found an ancient coastline.

The depths of the Black Sea are now made up of dense salt water devoid of oxygen. It is believed that any ancient remains down there may be perfectly preserved because there are no microbes to eat them.

In the summer of 2000, Bob Ballard, the sea explorer who found the Titanic, launched an expedition in the Black Sea to search for shipwrecks and ancient settlements destroyed as the great flood hit. He was also due to search for Noah's Ark — a mission carried out, so far in vain, by hundreds of climbers on 16,854ft Mount Ararat.

The snow-capped peak of Mount Ararat in modern-day Turkey — said to be the place where Noah's Ark came to rest as the flood water began to subside. A host of expeditions has climbed the mountain attempting to find traces of the ark. Aerial surveys have been done. None have found anything

A horde of animals prepares to board the ark two by two in this painting by 16th Century artist Francesco Bassano

...Timeline...

6000 Wheat and barley are cultivated for first time while pigs, cattle, sheep and goats are domesticated; Date of the first known pottery (Anatolia, now Turkey) — woollen textiles used there too; Bricks begin to be used.

Noah releases dove from the ark to see how far the flood has receded. This mosaic is from Venice's Basilica of San Marco

THE Sun

Thursday, February 18, 5498BC

THOUGHT: POUR FOOL

It's raining, it's pouring, the old man is sawing..

Zoo's coming with me . . . elephants, camels, giraffes and a host of other animals board Noah's ark in pairs as rain continued to fall last night   Picture: PETER PATTER

NUTTY NOAH FINISHES OFF WOODEN ARK

By CLAUD BURST

ANOTHER SUN EXCLUSIVE

A MAN called Noah is building a huge ark to save himself, his family and the entire animal kingdom from a flood he claims is about to devastate the world.

The 599-year-old dad of three says

God has warned him that the downpour which began yesterday will go on for 40 days and nights, killing all life on Earth.

He says the Almighty gave him the exact dimensions of his giant three-deck

wooden boat. It will be 450ft long, 75ft wide and 45ft deep, with a side door and a roof.

Noah was hard at work building it yesterday — and mating pairs of each animal species were being herded on board. Noah

told The Sun that God is furious about mankind's corruption and has decided to take drastic action.

But the supreme being has chosen to spare Noah and his family because he likes them.

Last night Noah's wife, their sons Shem, Ham and Japeth and their wives are all boarding the ship.

Today's Weather — Page 36

SNOOTY UNICORNS SHUN SANCTUARY OFFER - Pages 4&5

1,833,239 DAYS TO GO

Farmers in south-east Asia began to grow mangos around 5000. Elsewhere, irrigation was being used for the first time

...Timeline...

5000 First farming in Britain, introduced by immigrants — they use stone axes, antler combs and pottery and till the soil with flint tools. They also bury their dead in communal graves, some on tombs made of stone, others under large mounds of earth; Farmers in Mesopotamia (the area that is now eastern Syria, south-eastern Turkey and most of Iraq) use irrigation; Rice is farmed for first time, in Ganges Valley, India; Millet grown in China; Mangos in south-east Asia; Corn in Mexico; Date of the earliest Egyptian settlements.

Rice was farmed (top) in India's Ganges Valley about 5000 — while corn (below) was cultivated in Mexico

Flint and stone tools like those used to till the land

5000 BC

FARMING IN BRITAIN

FARMING was introduced to Britain about 5000BC — probably by settlers who had crossed from continental Europe.

It was an innovation that came late to these islands, arriving some 2,000 years after the peoples of the Middle East first started using tools of flint and stone to work the soil.

Some archaeologists believe the first farming may have taken place as early as 10,000BC. Wheat, barley and rice were among the first crops.

Whatever the true date, the development of farming completely altered man's relationship with the world around him — and changed the face of the planet forever.

Man's transition from a race of hunters and food-gathers to food producers was not rapid, instead taking place over thousands of years.

The first Stone Age farmers probably began by simply noticing which wild plants were edible and conserving them.

At some stage they learned to take the seeds of these plants and replant them in areas which had been cleared of other vegetation. The earliest farm tools were probably simple axes made of stone and flint.

With these the farmer could shape branches into digging sticks and eventually into early ploughs that scored the surface of the ground so seeds could be effectively planted.

To grow crops successfully the farmer needed access to water. In Europe this was not a problem — there was adequate rainfall to water the crops.

But in Egypt and Mesopotamia farmers depended on the annual flooding of rivers like the Nile and the Euphrates to irrigate the soil.

Most early farmers kept animals for meat as well as raising crops.

Their first herds were probably built by capturing young animals from wild herds of goats and sheep.

The earliest farmers lived together in small villages surrounded by fields.

These villages were often abandoned as fields lost their fertility because they were over-farmed.

A young mother grinds wheat using two slabs of stone. Archaeologists believe wheat, barley and rice were the first crops cultivated by the earliest farmers

WOOLLEN CLOTHES

NO ONE knows who were the first people to use wool, although the evidence points to those living in Anatolia in modern-day Turkey some 8,000 years ago.

Scholars think it is likely that ancient man first simply wore the skins of sheep before discovering it was possible to make a yarn from the tough outer covering. Nomadic peoples were among the first to make widespread use of wool — using it for clothes and tents.

These same nomads also invented carpets by knotting together wool and linen. Fragments of woollen fabrics have been found in the tombs of ancient Egyptians and Babylonians.

THE Sun

Tuesday, August 3, 5023BC

THOUGHT: HERE WE GROW

WE'VE GONE FARMY BARMY

Craze grips Britain

By BOBBY BIO

BRITAIN is in the grip of a great new game — called farming.

Players, known as farmers, begin by digging furrows in the earth.

Then they push the seeds of plants like corn into the little trenches, before covering them over with dirt. The first farmer to grow some crops is the winner.

But some people believe the craze is getting out of control. One tribal elder said: "People are playing this game all day when they should be out hunting. If this goes on we'll have nothing to eat."

Top of the crops — Page Six

Mum, can I have a Grain Boy . . . another youngster hooked on the farming craze. Kids all over the country are spending their pocket money on wheat

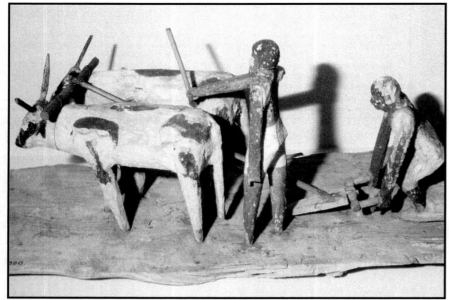

An ancient Egyptian model of men ploughing with oxen. The first plough was used about 4000. This model from about 2000 is one of the earliest depictions of ploughing

...Timeline...

4800 Mexicans cultivate squash, chili peppers and avocados; Citrus fruits being grown in various parts of the world.

4500 Egyptians bury dead with first known written documents; Inventor in Ur, Sumeria, makes a harp; Evidence of managed woodlands in Britain.

4400 Date of the first loom, in Egypt.

4000 Population spurt in Mesopotamia leads to first towns; The plough used for first time; Inventions of the bridge, drums and make-up all around this time; Earliest known British communities begin to spring up.

3900 People of Britain begin building ceremonial ditch-enclosed earthworks, like Durrington Walls in Wiltshire.

3600 Rough date for the first use of bronze, in south-west Asia.

3500 Walled cities built in China; Britain's first long barrows and chambered tombs — Waylands Smithy long barrow near Uffington, Oxfordshire, built around now; Egyptians invent a plywood.

Early bronze art. The metal was first used about 3600

3500BC
INVENTION OF THE WHEEL

THE wheel is probably the single greatest invention in history. Its importance to the development of mankind — and its influence on our world today — is incalculably huge.

Aside from forming the basis of most forms of transport on land, it is a device essential to a vast range of machines.

The wheel has ended up dictating the very look of the world, giving rise to road systems which shape our cities.

It has been assumed that the wheel was invented in Sumeria around 3500BC, the approximate date of a clay tablet discovered there on which a wheeled sledge had been sketched.

Wheels were used as turntables to make pottery in the same area at the time, though it is unclear which came first.

Mankind is thought to have previously shifted heavy objects by putting them on a sledge and rolling it over a series of round logs placed beneath.

As the object moved towards the last few logs, those at the start of the series were picked up and placed at the end, thus allowing the load to continue its slow progress.

With wear, the central portions of the logs became thinner than the edges, which brought an unexpected benefit.

As the laws of physics dictate, the rotating of the thinner area by the sledge turned the log's thicker ends much faster than had the entire log been thick. It therefore covered a greater distance with less effort.

Thus, man realised that the most efficient shape for the log was to pare it down to a thin "axle" with thick ends.

The next development was that the sledge, which had previously rolled freely over the logs, was loosely fixed to the axle using pegs, which meant that for the first time the axle and its ends, and the sledge, were able to roll along as one unit.

Next, the turning axle was fixed to the sledge in a more permanent arrangement. Later still it was realised that the axle could be fixed in place, immovably, beneath the sledge, while its ends were allowed to spin independently. And this was the true birth of the wheel.

The impact of the invention was dramatic. Horse-drawn carts, with wheels made from three carved planks clamped together, replaced sledges as the premium mode of transport.

Where once a horse had dragged a sledge behind it, straining against the friction of the sledge on the ground, it could now pull a cart containing several people with ease.

People began to travel more widely, from village to village, trading and exchanging information and services. The wheel brought about a revolution in agriculture, being a much more efficient use of the strength of a horse or ox.

The next major advance came around 1,500 years later when sections of the wheel were cut out and replaced with spokes attached to a central hub and an outer rim.

This had the advantage of significantly reducing the vehicle's weight and was particularly useful for war chariots which needed to be light and manoeuverable.

Eventually, iron rims were developed which became the first "tyres".

Later, around 100BC, bearings were first used to make the wheels run more smoothly.

Wheels, of course, ran most efficiently on purpose-built roads — and the Romans became master road-builders. Nowadays, roads dominate the landscape of the developed world — all thanks to the wheel.

Transport was not the only aspect of human life the wheel revolutionised.

A wheel and axle arrangement is found in most mechanical devices, from windmills to doorknobs and from mechanical clocks to round kitchen taps.

Mexican farmers began to grow chili peppers and avacados around 4800

Citrus fruits like lemons and limes were cultivated in various regions from 4800

Modern reconstructions of some of the earliest wooden wheels. Archaeological evidence suggests that the first wheel was invented in Sumeria around 3500BC

THE Sun

Thursday, October 19, 3468BC

THOUGHT: REVOLUTIONARY

YOU GET TO ROLL WITH IT

It's fat, it's round, it rolls along the ground . . . the new 'wheel'

Miracle wheel may be answer to world's transport headache

A NEW device known as a "wheel" was last night being hailed as the answer to the world's transport problems.

The round wooden objects can be loosely placed at either end of an axle and allowed to spin.

When the axle is fixed to the bottom of a sledge, for example, the

By MILES OMETER

wheels allow the entire contraption to roll along at considerable speed.

Several people can sit on top of the sledge and be carried along.

The wheeled device can cover 100 yards in a fraction of the time it currently takes for an ox to drag a sledge the same distance.

The knock-on effect of this is that

people might now be able to travel further than ever before.

Trips to the next settlement could be done in a **DAY.**

Safety campaigners last night warned that the wheel's circular design seemed short-sighted. One said: "Rolling along is all very well, but how do you stop? No one seems to have given this any thought."

Ken Gibson's View —
Sun Wheels, Page 68

VORSPRUG UG UGNIK
(as we say in the late mesolithic era)

THEY MUST BE ROUND THE BEND

By KEN GIBSON, Wheels Correspondent

THE wheel is certainly a bright idea. But one of the big problems with bright ideas is some poor devil has to try them out.

It's only when he ends up looking like something you'd feed to your dog that the little design flaws suddenly become crystal clear.

Now don't get me wrong. I think the concept of attaching a device to the four corners of your sled so it can move faster is brilliant. But why must these wheels be round?

Even the losing finalist of the annual village idiots' saliva-drooling contest knows round things have an alarming tendency to roll away. Especially when they come to a downhill bit.

Picture the scene. You decide to take the family out for a Sunday afternoon's sledding in the country — with your brand new round wheels in place.

You attach a couple of thoroughbred oxen to the front, load up the missus, the toddlers and gran — and you're off.

With a crack of the whip the oxen

Square, star or triangular wheels are much safer

surge forward like the finely-tuned athletes they are. It's a bit hairy at first because the wheels let the sled travel four times as fast as usual. But once you get used to gran screaming, it all becomes quite fun. Then you come to a downhill stretch.

It's only when the sled actually overtakes the oxen that you realise things are getting out of hand. You try lightening the load by chucking gran out, but that makes it go faster still.

Luckily, you are brought to a halt by a conveniently-positioned tree. You escape with bruises. Unfortunately, your wife will be spending the rest of her life wearing her nose as a hat.

See? It's obvious that where wheels are concerned, round is unsound. But that's not to say other shapes wouldn't fit the bill. A **TRIANGULAR** wheel is much safer. However, each of its sides slams to the ground with great force, giving an uncomfortable ride.

An **OVAL** wheel gives a much smoother sensation. But the oval's long sides and round ends cause a pronounced rocking motion guaranteed to make the kids sea-sick.

A **STAR-SHAPE** is too bumpy on firm ground. But it is useful on rough-terrain sleds needing extra grip to stop them sliding in snow or thick mud.

For me, the pick of the bunch is the **SQUARE** wheel. It gives reasonable speed, a more comfy ride than the triangle and it won't roll off when you park it.

OK, it's not as nippy as a round wheel. But surely this is outweighed by the fact you can negotiate a slight incline without the entire family needing a change of underwear.

So please, let's think again about these new round devices — before the wheels really **DO** come off.

And if anyone tries to persuade you to fit a circular set of wheels to your sled, just tell them they are talking complete round objects.

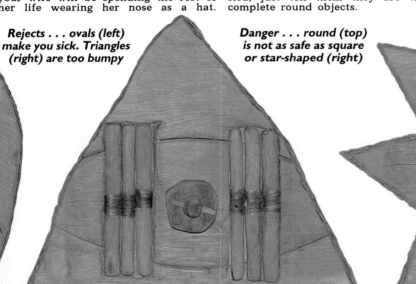

Rejects . . . ovals (left) make you sick. Triangles (right) are too bumpy

Danger . . . round (top) is not as safe as square or star-shaped (right)

CART, THE UNSTOPPABLE OX MACHINE

HOLD on to your hats, speed-freaks because here comes the Cart — a vehicle that is even FASTER than a wild horse.

The amazing sled-on-wheels is the swiftest thing to hit the transport world since man first set light to a donkey's tail.

The Cart, which features a set of the prototype round wheels, has been produced amid the utmost secrecy in Sumeria.

During trials it is said to have reached TEN TIMES walking speed. The test driver, an experienced sled racer, even developed a nose bleed because of the

extreme acceleration. The Sun is the only paper to be given a sneak preview of the Cart, which is powered by a pair of specially-trained water buffalo.

One member of the design team said: "We have a few minor problems to sort out, like steering and stopping.

"At the moment it only goes in straight lines and to stop you have to aim at a wall or large rock then leap clear just before impact. But this is definitely the future of transport. In a few years we'll all be driving a Cart."

Gee whizz . . . cart goes at ten times walking pace

2750 BC

THE SUMERIANS

THE Sumerians were among the most inventive of ancient civilisations.

They lived in the fertile valleys between the Tigris and Euphrates rivers in an area which is today Iraq, Kuwait and northern Saudi Arabia.

They were a brilliant people who built the first real cities, had relatively advanced religions and legal systems, invented calendars — and at some time around 3100BC developed writing.

The earliest surviving Sumerian writings are records of the amount of grain kept in storehouses.

The earliest "words" are little more than simplified pictures of the things they represent — known as pictographs.

The Sumerians made these records by scratching on wet clay with pieces of reed. The clay was then allowed to dry until it was rock-hard.

Over the years the Sumerians improved and expanded their writing skills, replacing the pictographs with a type of shorthand made up of a series of wedge-shaped marks.

The Sumerians may also have been the first people to brew beer. Surviving clay tablets mention more than 20 varieties. One type, called sikaru, was used in religious ceremonies to pay honour to the gods. The Sumerians made their beer by soaking wheat and barley in water, then flavouring it with dates and honey.

It was usually drunk from a communal pot, with drinkers sucking up the liquid through reeds. Wealthy Sumerians used beer-drinking reeds made of gold.

Archaeologists have discovered the remains of a large government-run brewery in the ruins of the small Sumerian city of Ur. Ur and its neighbouring cities of Lagash and Eridu were constantly at war with one another — a fact that led the Sumerians also to develop the first proper armies.

A mosaic found in the ruins of Ur shows soldiers with spears and charging chariots. But their armies could not save them from their more aggressive neighbours like the Akkadians, who conquered them around 2000BC.

However, Sumerian civilisation was so powerful the conquerors adopted the government, economy, religion and writing skills of the conquered.

TOWER OF BABEL

THE Biblical story of the Tower of Babel seems to be an attempt by the writers of the Old Testament to explain why different languages are spoken all over the world.

The book of Genesis, Chapter 11 Verses 1-9, tells how Noah's descendants decided to make a name for themselves by building a fabulous tower on the Shinar plain in Babylonia.

It was intended to be so high it would reach into heaven.

God was furious. According to Genesis, he said: "They are one people and they have all one language and this is only the beginning of what they will do. Nothing that they propose to do will now be impossible for them."

God then caused the builders to speak in different languages so they could not understand each other.

The building work ended unfinished and the builders were scattered all over the world, each speaking a different language. "Babel" gave rise to the English word "babble."

A terracotta model of a Sumerian war chariot, dating from sometime after 3000

Head of a Sumerian mace — inscribed with the words "To Shara, beloved son of Inanna"

...Timeline...

3400 Pottery made with wheel in Sumeria.

3200 Earliest legible documents — and a lunar calendar — emerge in Mesopotamia; Cities emerge in Egypt, where black ink is invented.

3100 Pictographic writing invented in Sumer and hieroglyphics in Egypt; Building starts at Stonehenge in Wiltshire, the phase known as Stonehenge I.

3000 Start of Minoan civilisation in Crete; The Sumerians invent a type of soap; Glass is invented in western Asia; Date of the first known button, found in the Indus Valley, northern India; Egypt and Mesopotamia are both making boats from reeds; Egyptians are weaving from flax; Chinese and Mesopotamians using herbs for medicine; Potatoes cultivated in Peru, South America; Egyptians have fish ponds; One of Britain's earliest stone circles, at Castlerigg, Cumbria, is begun; Chambered tomb built at Pentre Ifan, Dyfed; Beeswax candles are in use in Egypt and Crete.

2800 Gilgamesh is king in Mesopotamia.

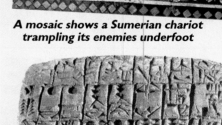

A mosaic shows a Sumerian chariot trampling its enemies underfoot

A pictograph tablet from ancient Mesopotamia. The tablet's text refers to metal drinking vessels

Impression taken from an ancient Sumerian seal. It is thought to represent the Sumerian hero Gilgamesh fighting lions and bulls

A Sumerian bill, from about 2800, for the sale of a field and house. The total was paid in silver

THE SuN

Friday, November 5, 2749BC

THOUGHT: HIC HIC HOORAY

Fabulous new 'skyscraper' to reach heaven

By BOB DeBILDER, Architecture Correspondent

AN amazing high-rise tower is being built as a kind of "ladder" to heaven.

The "skyscraper" will be so tall it will reach right up into the celestial kingdom.

Managers of the Tower of Babel on the Shinar plain in Babylonia have not yet revealed how many stairs one will need to climb to get to the top. And they are putting a brave face on a string of problems which are plaguing the project.

Probably the most serious is that many of the builders have begun for no apparent reason to speak in different languages — and cannot make themselves understood to the others.

A spokesman at the site said: "This is obviously a concern and we don't quite know why it's happened. But we're determined to carry on to ensure our place in history."

Towering Achievement — Page 15

BEER IS HERE

Brew's company . . Sumerian lads on town last night

(and so is writing)

By BUD WEISER and ROLAND ROCK

GENIUSES in Sumeria have invented an astonishing miracle drink called beer.

Made from a mixture of water, barley and dates, it allegedly makes people deliriously happy.

It is also said to make those who drink it witty, clever, brave and attractive to the opposite sex.

But some say gulping large quantities of the liquid has a strange side-effect — loss of memory.

To help drinkers cope with this, the beer boffins have come up with another brilliant idea — which they call writing.

This involves representing things or people by carving small pictures of them on bits of clay.

By using this technique, people can "write down" important information — then drink large quantities of beer without worrying about memory loss.

Bigger Than The Wheel — Page 9

963,233 DAYS TO GO

2639 BC

THE FIRST PYRAMID

THE Step Pyramid at Saqqara in Egypt is thought to be the first monumental stone building in the world. The massive tomb, built for the Pharaoh Djoser, is also the prototype for all the pyramids that followed.

Before the Step Pyramid the Pharaohs had been entombed in large rectangular bunkers made of sun-dried mud bricks. They were known as mastabas.

It is thought that Step Pyramid was originally built as a normal mastaba, but was gradually enlarged by adding further rectangular bunkers, one on top of the other, until it consisted of six "boxes." By the time it was finished the Step Pyramid was 200ft high. Originally the surface was covered in a smooth white limestone so that it reflected the sun.

The brains behind the Step Pyramid was Djoser's chief minister Imhotep.

He is said to have been an architect, doctor and astronomer.

In later centuries he was revered as a minor god by the Egyptians.

The tomb of Djoser himself was about 90ft under ground and reached by a vertical shaft.

Its entrance was sealed with a giant slab of granite weighing about three tons.

When the site was excavated, archaeologists discovered a statue of Djoser in the burial chamber itself. It was damaged but still recognisable.

The concept of the Step Pyramid was revolutionary — but it did not last.

Scholars believe only one other Step Pyramid was built before the first "true" smooth-sided pyramid was constructed. This is thought to have been the so-called Bent Pyramid, just south of Saqqara at Dashur.

This was built for the Pharaoh Snefru, who is said to have died in 2565BC.

It is called the Bent Pyramid because the lower half slopes up at a sharper angle that the top half — giving the building a twisted look. It is thought that the pyramid was constructed like this because the builders feared that it might collapse once they were half-way through the job — and decided to reduce the height for safety.

Snefru was the great builder of the Egyptian world — being the proud owner of three full-size pyramids and two smaller ones.

The building of the pyramids proves that Egypt had both a thriving economy and a strong government around 2600BC.

The construction of such huge monuments required an effective administration to ensure a ready supply of workers and raw materials. Items found in the tombs also show a high level of skill among craftsmen.

The gateway to the enclosure of the Step Pyramid at Saqqara. The huge tomb, built for the Pharaoh Djoser, is the prototype for all the pyramids of Egypt. The pyramid itself in 200ft high and was originally covered in white sandstone

A statue of the Pharaoh Djoser from the burial chamber at Saqqara which is 90ft under ground

Sickles were used by the Sumerians from about 2750

...Timeline...

2750 Sumerians invent the sickle for harvesting grain.

2700 Chinese grow rhubarb – for medicine; Building of massive and mysterious 12-storey mound of earth and chalk rubble, known as Silbury Hill, Salisbury Plain — it is the largest prehistoric structure in Europe.

Silbury Hill, built around 2700, is the largest prehistoric structure in Europe — equivalent to a 12-storey building. Its purpose is unknown

THE Sun

Wednesday, December 28, 2639BC   THOUGHT: DEAD DAFT

LOONY TOMBS

Egyptians put up a 'Pointy' in the desert

BARMY Egyptians have put up a huge building that rises to a point — in the middle of the desert.

And as if that's not mad enough they plan to put a dead bloke inside it!

The 200ft high building, which has been dubbed a Pointy, has been built for Pharaoh Djoser.

It is made up of six rectangular buildings piled on top of one another — each one smaller than the last.

The Pointy has taken years to construct and has cost the Pharaoh a small fortune.

But now it is finished it will remain

By MAUDE SOLEUM

EMPTY — until Djoser dies. He will then be put in a sealed room at the centre of the building and surrounded by lots of gold and precious gems.

The Pointy is the brainchild of Pharaoh's adviser Imhotep, allegedly the cleverest man in Egypt.

MODERN

A spokesman for British hut giants Wattle & Daub said: "It's very flash, but it'll never catch on.

"This Pointy is typical modern architecture — I bet the bloke who designed it lives in a lovely old hut."

Pharaoh To Anointy Pointy — Page Two

Genius . . Pointy chief Imhotep

2500 BC

TAMING OF THE HORSE

Carvings on an ancient wine storage jar show a group of Scythian nomads taming a wild horse. The Scythians, who lived on the Russian steppes, were expert horsemen. The storage jar dates from around the 6th century BC

EARLY humans were interested in horses for only one reason — food. At first they hunted herds of wild horses along with boar and deer, the other staples of their diet.

There is little clear evidence to suggest exactly when man first began to realise the horse was more useful as transport.

Some scholars believe that the remains of more than 50 horses found at a Stone Age site in the Ukraine suggest that people living there may have ridden horses 6,000 years ago.

However, the evidence is inconclusive. Similarly, it is far from clear whether man tamed the horse so it could pull a wheeled cart — or be ridden.

Traditionally, historians believed horses were used as draught animals for hundreds if not thousands of years before they were first ridden by Central Asian nomads about 2500BC.

BUT recent research has suggested man may have been making bridles to control a ridden horse more than 500 years before the first known use of the wheel.

Certainly, by 2000BC tame horses were a feature of societies from Asia to Europe.

Almost inevitably, the horse had its greatest impact in warfare.

The great warrior nations of the 2nd millennium BC dominated the middle east because they had chariots. These allowed one or more bowmen to fire from a relatively stable platform while a driver steered.

True mounted cavalrymen are seen in Egyptian art as early as about 1400BC but they did not begin to replace the chariot until about 800BC.

...Timeline...

2600 Scribes are being employed in Egypt.

2590 Egypt's King Cheops builds the great pyramid at Giza and the Sphinx — both still top tourist attractions.

2550 The great pyramid of Khufu is constructed.

2500 Start of the Bronze Age; Arrival in Britain of so-called Beaker folk from the Low Countries and the middle Rhine; Cotton is grown and woven into cloth in Peru and the Indus Valley, India; Egypt and Asia growing figs, grapes, pomegranates and dates; Egypt has domesticated the cat and is using wind instruments for music and papyrus for paper; Olive trees cultivated in Crete; "Henge" monuments appear in Britain; Banking begins in Babylon (modern-day Iraq), with temples and palaces providing safe places for storing grain, then tools and precious metals.

The Great Pyramid and the Sphinx (left) both date from 2590

Dates and grapes were being grown in Egypt from 2500

THE BEAKER PEOPLE

MYSTERY surrounds the origins of the Beaker People — so named because of the geometrically-patterned drinking cups found in their graves. Some scholars believe they were a wave of immigrants who crossed the North Sea from modern-day Belgium and Holland.

Others think they were a group who had always lived here, but had simply developed new ideas and new methods of doing things.

Whatever the truth, the Beaker People made their first appearance in Britain around 2500BC.

They are thought to have been farmers who lived in huts grouped together in small villages. Historians believe they were the first Britons with a knowledge of metalwork. Copper daggers attributed to them have been found at various sites.

THE Sun

Friday, January 1, 2501 BC

THOUGHT: HERE COMES THE RIDE

STEADY NEDDY

Bloke tames a horse and rides it about

By STEWART SINQUIRY

THIS is the moment when a daredevil climbed on a horse's back — and RODE it.

The stunned nag stood up on two legs and took a few steps.

Then it spun round violently — sending its rider flying to the ground.

The embarrassed rider, the first man to try this stunt, said: "If I can persuade it to keep all four legs on the ground and behave itself I think we'll be on to a winner."

Does The Buck Stop Here? — Page 11

COUNTDOWN TO CHRIST

733,556 DAYS TO GO

The Hale-Bopp comet (pictured here over Arizona) caused wonderment in 1997, as it must have done in 2200BC

Standing stone at the Avebury Circle in Wiltshire, which was built around 2300BC and is popular tourist spot

2010 BC
STONEHENGE

STONEHENGE is the most famous, and the most spectacular, of all Britain's prehistoric monuments. But don't be fooled by our light-hearted page opposite — it was never meant to be a millennium dome! In fact its real purpose is unknown, and still hotly debated.

Even today the site is breath-taking — and yet it is a shadow of its former glory, having been battered by the elements over three millennia, smashed up by the Romans and raided over the last few hundred years by builders hampered by the lack of natural stone in the area.

The technical and physical achievement of building Stonehenge almost defies belief.

The fact that some of the massive stone blocks were dragged from mountains 240 miles away proves that it can only have been the work of a sophisticated society capable of organising a large workforce.

And the design skills needed to erect and shape the monument, using only the crudest of tools, seem amazingly advanced for the societies of 5,000 to 3,000 years ago.

The history of the Stonehenge site, eight miles north-west of Salisbury, Wiltshire, is known from the extensive archaeology carried out there, particularly over the last 50 years.

We know it was built in three stages over about 1,500 years, beginning around 3100BC with the phase now known as Stonehenge I.

That consisted of a circular ditch 320ft round, which the Neolithic Britons dug out using deer antlers.

They erected two upright stones to form an entrance. One is now known as the Slaughter Stone, and still exists. Just inside the inner bank of the ditch they dug a circle of 56 holes — known as the Aubrey Holes and named after John Aubrey, the 17th Century historian who found them — and drove wooden posts into them.

The Stonehenge I site was used for 500 years before it reverted to scrubland.

Centuries later, around 2100, work began on Stonehenge II, which gave the site a drastic new look and required a phenomenal effort of manpower.

Around 80 pillars of bluestone weighing as much as four tons each were dragged 240 miles there over land, sea and river from the Preseli Mountains in south-west Wales.

It is not known how this was done — it has been speculated that gangs of workers made rafts and dragged them across land, or somehow pushed the stones forward on a rolling platform made from rounded logs. Whatever the method, the distance, time and effort involved are simply staggering. The pillars were erected in the centre of the site to form two circles, though they were never finished.

A straight, two-mile long ditch-lined track now called The Avenue led north-east from the site's entrance.

About 2000BC marked the start of the Stonehenge III phase, which saw the dismantling of the two stone circles from 100 years earlier and the erection of the gigantic sarsen stones, the remains of which are seen at the site today.

These stones, up to 30ft long and weighing 50 tons, were brought from the Marlborough Downs 20 miles north. Thirty stones were initially placed upright, forming a circle, and were capped with other blocks of stone. This is known as a "post and lintel" arrangement.

Each lintel was fixed to the next using tongue-and-groove joints, while they were also fixed to the uprights below them using dovetail joints — both techniques still in use by modern craftsmen.

The lintels were meticulously hammered so that they were curved and would form a circle. Of the 30 uprights, 17 are still standing. Inside this circle, a horseshoe-shaped formation of five pairs of larger stones was built, once again with each pair linked by a lintel.

The bluestones which were already on the site were rearranged into circular and horseshoe shapes inside the circle and horseshoe made up by the larger sarsen stones.

Various minor adjustments were made to Stonehenge over the next 500 years. The site was still in use as late as 1100BC — and evidence uncovered in July 2000 showed that it may have been an execution site as late as 690AD.

Even Stonehenge experts admit it is unlikely we will ever know what its real purpose was. It may have been a place of worship — but claims that it was built for druids are false since it pre-dates them by many centuries.

One intriguing aspect of the mystery is the discovery that the axis of the site (i.e. a straight line drawn through the circle and up The Avenue) points to the position where the sun rises at the summer solstice.

Two theories have sprung from this. One is that the early Britons were sun worshippers. The other is that Stonehenge was a remarkably complex "computer" which could predict the onset of the seasons and even eclipses of the sun and moon.

It is fairly certain that we will never know for sure.

...Timeline...

2400 Indian writers use engraved seals to identify themselves.

2300 Construction of Britain's biggest stone circle, the "Avebury Ring" in Wiltshire.

2296 World's first empire founded, by Sargon I of Agade, southern Mesopotamia.

2200 Minoans build magnificent palaces at Knossos and Phaestus, Crete; The Hale-Bopp comet visits Earth for last time before its much-publicised re-appearance in 1997AD.

2136 An eclipse of the sun is recorded by Chinese astronomers.

2100 Building begins on the second phase of Stonehenge — Stonehenge II.

2010 Rough date for its final version, Stonehenge III.

Carved head of Sargon, founder of the world's first empire (2296)

THE Sun

Friday, September 9, 2010BC

THOUGHT: DISASTER ZONE

How it should look . . . pillars are meant to support state-of-the-art roof

SHAMBLES

● 'Dome' in disarray at Stonehenge

● It'll never be ready for New Year do

● 1,100 yrs' work .. and still no roof

● VIPs face huge queue for tickets

THE Millennium Dome project at Stonehenge can today be exposed by The Sun as a monumental shambles.

An undercover Sun reporter found the venue for Britain's New Year's celebrations in disarray — even though chiefs have had 1,100 years to plan it.

With just three months to go before the big night only the roof's support-

By MEG ALITH, Buildings Correspondent

ing pillars seem to be in place. Some of those appear to have fallen over and are too heavy to put back upright.

There is absolutely no sign of the much-hyped roof itself. Nor is there any sign of the themed "zones" which are said to have been put together at enormous cost.

One insider at the Wiltshire site said: "It's been a disaster from start to finish — the project was obviously given to the wrong people. It'll take a mira-

cle for them to get it done on time."

There was further bad news last night for Dome organisers the NMEC, the Neolithic Monuments Erection Corporation. None of the VIPs or "ordinary people" invited to the December 31 bash have received their tickets because of an organisational mix-up.

Thousands are likely to have to queue for as much as three hours in the freezing cold to collect their tickets before catching a cart to the venue.

The "Dome" has been in the making since the **LAST** millennium. Two previ-

ous versions were thrown out before the plans were finally approved. Last night the NMEC insisted it **WOULD** be ready on time.

A spokesman said: "It was always going to be a long process, what with having to drag those dirty great slabs of stone hundreds of miles across hill and dale without any technology to speak of.

"But we're confident we'll make the deadline and the Dome will be something the country can be proud of."

Dome Bet On It — Pages 4 and 5

712,011 DAYS TO GO

Watermelon was first cultivated in Africa about 2000

1950BC

SODOM & GOMORRAH

GOD'S destruction of the twin cities of Sodom and Gomorrah is one the earliest Bible stories. According to the Book of Genesis, God decided to wipe out the cities and their inhabitants because of their wickedness and sexual immorality.

Apparently, there was only one righteous man among all the citizens. His name was Lot, the brother of Abraham.

God decided to spare Lot and sent a couple of angels to warn him to leave his home in Sodom along with his wife and two teenage daughters.

The angels told Lot to warn any other relatives he had to get out of the city. He duly visited some of his male relatives but they refused to listen to him. The next morning, the angels hurried Lot and his family out of Sodom. They told them to flee to the mountains and not look back.

Lot was scared at the thought of having to survive in the mountains, so he begged the angels to let him go to the small city of Zoar nearby. The angels agreed.

As the family fled, fire and brimstone began to rain down on both cities. But Lot's wife could not resist turning round to watch the destruction and was immediately turned into a pillar of salt.

Biblical scholars believe Sodom and Gomorrah were situated at the southern end of the Dead Sea.

Some historians think the Bible story may represent the cities' destruction by an earthquake some time around 1900BC.

Lot flees from the burning Sodom with his teenage daughters while his wife is turned into a pillar of salt as she looks back to see the destruction

A modern tea plantation in Haputale, Sri Lanka. Tea was first cultivated by farmers in India some time after 2000

...Timeline...

2000 Britain's population somewhere between 50,000 and 200,000; The spoked wheel is developed; Britons are making cloth and metal objects; Approximate date of the Clava cairns, magnificent neolithic burial chambers near Inverness, Scotland; Crete becomes leading power in Eastern Mediterranean, trading with Egypt and Syria; Hittites (from modern-day Turkey) begin 700-year period as main political power in Asia minor; First sails used on ships in Aegean; Bananas and tea cultivated in India; Watermelon cultivated in Africa; Rough date of the start of the Xia dynasty's reign in China. **1990** Egypt conquers Nubia (north-east Africa).

CHINA AND THE DUCK

THE domestication of the duck by the Chinese may be to blame for introducing flu to mankind. Around 2000BC the wild duck's main habitats were lakes in Siberia and the rice fields of southern China. But when the Chinese began to domesticate mallards for their eggs they set off an influenza timebomb.

Ducks are the biggest flu carriers in nature. And although it is believed impossible for them to pass the bird strain of the virus directly to humans, it is believed that they DID pass it on to the pigs they were kept alongside.

The pigs acted as a "vessel" in which the flu strain mutated so that it could be caught by humans.

FLUSHING TOILETS

THE world's first flushing loo was built at the spectacular palace of King Minos at Knossos on Crete around 1900BC. It had a wooden seat and a small reservoir beneath which held rain water, thought to have poured off the palace roof. It was partitioned off for privacy.

The four-storey palace was, in fact, a remarkable achievement in early plumbing, with under-floor terracotta pipes, four drainage systems and even gold and silver hot and cold taps over marble sinks.

The queen's bathroom had a 5ft tub which drained into a hole in the floor, which took the water into the main palace drain and then into a river.

The Clava cairns, stone age burial chambers near Inverness, were constructed around 2000

Farmers in India began growing bananas for first time in about 2000

THE Sun

Wednesday, August 17, 1951BC   **THOUGHT: SALT AND PEEPER**

They've quacked it . . ducks last night

Tamed at last!

Ducks captured by the Chinese

By LES EATEM

CHINA has tamed the duck, The Sun can sensationally reveal.

The elusive wild birds have been sighted waddling happily around ice fields and farms in the far-eastern country.

The Chinese are the world's first civilisation to attempt to domesticate the birds. It is believed they want them for their eggs. Ducks themselves may be edible too.

The birds, from Siberia, are being kept alongside other animals — which is causing alarm among health experts because ducks are the biggest flu carriers in nature.

Web Feat — see Page 15

Palace unveils new 'flushing loo' sensation

By PAUL DeCHAIN

THE first flushing toilet has been invented, it was dramatically announced last night.

The news was broken to a stunned world direct from the palace of Crete's King Minos, where the loo is installed.

The device is said to be centuries ahead of its time.

It has a wooden seat and a small reservoir beneath it that collects rain water which flows off the roof of the palace at Knossos.

It is even partitioned off for the user's privacy and convenience.

Last night loo makers were scrambling to get hold of the blueprints.

CITY OF SIN IN FLAMES

By CLARE CONSCIENCE and PRU MISCUOUS

THE fun-loving city of Sodom was destroyed by God yesterday — because he was sick and tired of its citizens' sinful ways.

He poured fire and an unpleasant-smelling substance called brimstone on to the city until it was razed to the ground.

Only the city's gatekeeper Lot, his wife and their two teenage daughters escaped the inferno. They are thought to have been forewarned.

Minutes later Sodom's twin city of Gomorrah was devastated in a similar attack.

God has apparently been furious with the people of Sodom and Gomorrah for many years because of their lewd and immoral behaviour.

Undercover reporters from The Sun revealed last month how many of Sodom's leading citizens regularly held boozy wife-swapping parties.

Last night an angel of the Lord confirmed that the deity was responsible for the cataclysm. He said: "I cannot say too much for legal reasons. But the Lord's vengeance is swift and terrible."

● **LOT'S** wife turned into a pile of salt just minutes after fleeing Sodom, it was claimed last night. A witness said she was transformed after glancing back at the burning city.

Wall paintings from the palace of Knossos, Crete, showing a boy vaulting a bull (top) and dolphins (below). The palace was destroyed by earthquake around 1700

1628 BC

ATLANTIS LEGEND

THE story of Atlantis, the island city that disappeared beneath the waves, has fascinated people throughout history.

The Greeks believed it had been a large island situated in the Western Ocean near the pillars of Hercules — their name for the straits of Gibraltar.

They said that Atlantis was engulfed when the sea rose following an earthquake.

The disaster is said to have taken place over a single day and night.

The tale was certainly taken seriously in ancient Greece, so much so that Atlantis features in two surviving works by the great Athenian philosopher Plato.

In the first, called Timaeus, an Egyptian priest says the island of Atlantis was huge — larger, in fact, than Asia Minor and North Africa combined.

He claims that around 10,000BC the people of Atlantis had an advanced civilisation.

The Egyptian says Atlantis ruled a vast empire that took in all of the lands around the Mediterranean.

In a second work, called Critias, Atlantis is represented in rather poetic terms as the perfect state — an ideal political institution to which man can now only aspire.

In Critias, Plato also tells how Atlantis was originally part of the kingdom of the sea god Poseidon.

Apparently, Poseidon fell in love with a woman named Cleito and built a home for her on top of a hill at the centre of the island.

The god surrounded the home with alternating rings of land and water to protect Cleito. Plato says that Cleito gave birth to five sets of twin boys. The island was divided among the boys, who became the founders of a splendid, sophisticated race.

But after centuries of peace, the people of Atlantis became greedy and smug and no longer paid the gods their due reverence.

Zeus, the chief of the gods, became so angry he decided to punish the people of Atlantis by destroying the island.

Critias also claims that a war was fought between Athens and Atlantis in the distant past.

In all, fewer than 20 pages in Plato's two works deal with the Atlantis story.

But such is the fascination of the subject, it was recently estimated that more than 25,000 books have been written on the Atlantis legend.

Today, some scientists believe the legend sprang from the destruction caused by a huge volcanic eruption on the Greek island of Thira, nowadays known as Santorini.

Much of the isle seems to have been destroyed in the catastrophe in 1628BC.

The modern island of Santorini is the rim of the volcano. The rest of the isle is still buried beneath the sea.

Santorini also has an abundance of volcanic ash which its modern inhabitants use to make cement. During their diggings they regularly turn up ancient ruins.

Some writers believe the Canary Islands, Crete or America to be the inspiration behind the legend.

...Timeline...

1800 Date of the earliest corset (seen on statue in Crete).

1750 Greeks arrive in the Balkans and the middle-east becomes a mass of warring dynasties; Northernmost Greenland is settled.

1749 Shamshi-Adad founds the Assyrian state (modern-day northern Iraq and south-eastern Turkey).

1728 Beginning of the reign of Hammurabi of Babylon — he establishes his famous code of law, including "eye for an eye"-style punishments, sections on ditch maintenance and various property laws with rules about gardens.

1700 Minoan palaces at Knossos and Phaestus are destroyed by earthquakes but both are rebuilt; Babylonians invent windmills which pump water for irrigating crops; Start of the reign of the Shang dynasty in China; Mathematicians in Egypt are using fractions.

1674 The Hyksos peoples from Asia Minor invade Egypt.

1628 Huge volcanic eruption on island of Thira in Aegean (probable basis for Atlantis legend).

A map supposedly showing the position of Atlantis — in the Atlantic Ocean between Africa and America. The map comes from a book dated 1678AD

THE Sun

WHERE IS ATLANTIS?

Sailor reports continent is missing

THE huge continent of Atlantis has mysteriously disappeared.

Atlantis, which has a population of many thousands, is a vast area of land in the Western Ocean.

It was first reported missing a week ago by a Greek sailor — but his claims were dismissed because he is known to have a drink problem.

But last night the Egyptian government admitted that its trading fleet,

By DONNA PLUGHOLE

which set out on a mission to Atlantis six weeks ago, has returned after being unable to find the island continent, ten times the size of Britain.

A spokesman said: "We know it was there three months ago because we sent them ten shiploads of sand they needed for building work.

"It's most strange — but it'll probably turn up eventually." The island is home to one of the world's most advanced civilisations and features a number of fabulous cities.

Scientists already have a number of theories about what has happened to Atlantis *(pictured below)*.

Some say it may have been engulfed by giant waves following a huge volcanic explosion.

Others think it is more likely to have been eaten by an enormous fish.

Find Atlantis And Win Diving Holiday For Two — Page 17

492,588 DAYS TO GO

1350BC

LEGEND OF ICARUS

A statue of the Athenian hero Theseus clubbing to death the Minotaur — a monster that was half bull, half man — after entering the labyrinth in Crete

Silkworms spinning cocoons on a loom. The Chinese began weaving with silk about 1500 but managed to keep the method used a secret for centuries

GREEK legend tells how Icarus was killed as he and his father Daedalus were attempting to fly to freedom after being imprisoned on the island of Crete.

Daedalus had made them both wings by sticking bird feathers together with wax.

The wings worked to perfection, but as father and son soared towards freedom Icarus got carried away and flew too close to the sun.

The intense heat melted the wax holding the feathers together — and Icarus plunged to his death.

The fatal flight is the climax of a dramatic tale set on ancient Crete at a time when it was ruled by the tyrannical King Minos.

According to legend, the sea god Poseidon had sent King Minos a white bull, with instructions that it was to be sacrificed to him.

When Minos refused to sacrifice the bull angry Poseidon made Minos's queen Pasiphaë fall in love with it. The result of the doomed love was that Pasiphaë gave birth to the minotaur — a monster that had the head of a bull and the body of a man.

Minos made the inventor Daedalus build a labyrinth and imprisoned the minotaur in it. The trapped beast was then fed on young men and women that Minos forced the city of Athens to send him in tribute.

Daedalus had been forbidden to tell anyone how to get out of the labyrinth — but he revealed the secret to Minos's daughter Ariadne.

When the Athenian hero Theseus arrived on the isle determined to stop the slaughter of his fellow citizens, Ariadne fell in love with him. She vowed to help him kill the minotaur.

Theseus crept into the labyrinth, beat the minotaur to death with his club and made his escape with Ariadne's aid. Minos was furious.

He realised that Daedalus must have revealed the secret to someone and promptly imprisoned him and his son Icarus on the island.

The cunning inventor made his makeshift wings so they could fly away.

But he warned Icarus not to get too near the sun.

The young man, however, was so delighted with his new powers that he forgot his father's words — and fell into the sea and drowned.

Daedalus managed to escape to Sicily, where he was given sanctuary.

THE HERETIC PHARAOH

PHARAOH Akhenaten abolished the age-old religion of Egypt and replaced it with worship of the sun. The traditional Egyptian religion included a bewildering array of gods — more than 60 have been identified.

When Akhenaten became pharaoh in 1352BC he decided to sweep this system away, replacing it with worship of the Aten — a sun god who had until then been a rather minor deity represented by a small disc. The Pharaoh closed the temples of all other gods and forbade their worship. Up to this point he had been known as Amenhotep IV. But in celebration of his new religion he changed his name to Akhenaten, which translates as Servant of the Aten.

Akhenaten reigned for 16 years, but on his death his new religion died with him and Egypt returned to its old gods.

Some modern historians believe Akhenaten's revolution was an attempt to curb the political power of Egypt's priests.

...Timeline...

1600 Beginning of Mycenaean civilisation in Greece.

1550 Date of the Rhind Papyrus, a mathematical "handbook" containing 85 problems, found in a tomb in Egypt.

1500 Various forms of writing emerge in China, Greece, Crete and Anatolia; Chinese begin weaving with silk; Egyptians wear sandals.

1493 Valley of Kings founded by Pharaoh Thutmosis I.

1482 Thutmosis begins to expand into Palestine.

1450 First literature in India; First sundial in use, in Egypt. Cretan power begins to wane.

1400 Rough date of the Belas Knap chambered tomb near Winchcombe, Gloucestershire — 38 skeletons were discovered there with burial artefacts; Rise to power in Greece of Myceneans; Alphabetic writing at Ugarit, Syria; Oldest known writing in China, on bones.

1380 First canal links Nile to Red Sea.

1370 Destruction of Knossos, Crete.

Two Egyptian carvings of the heretic Pharaoh Akhenaten, who ruled from 1352. On the left, he is seen with wife Nefertiti. On the right, he is pictured sacrificing to the Sun god

THE Sun

Saturday, July 10, 1350

THOUGHT: HOT OFF THE PRESS

THE Sun IS GOD
OFFICIAL

YOU always knew we were something special, folks. But now it's official — The Sun is GOD!

The all-conquering Egyptian Pharaoh Akhenaten, right, has instructed his people that from now on they must abandon all their other gods and worship The Sun exclusively.

In fact, Akhenaten — whose name translates as servant of The Sun — is so convinced of our wis-

By SUE PREME-BEING

dom and power that he plans to build temples for us all over his vast kingdom.

Now, we're not suggesting our readers should bow down before us and offer up prayers.

But in case you ever feel tempted by one of the rags published by our so-called rivals, just remember — we'll be watching!

But don't get too close, folks, or...

MELTDOWN

Man's first flight ends in tragedy as wings fall apart

Flightmare . . . Daedalus watches in horror yesterday as Icarus plunges towards sea

MAN'S first flight ended in disaster yesterday as a lad named Icarus died when his wings melted because he flew too near the sun.

Icarus, 19, and his dad Daedalus, 41, took to the air wearing fake wings made from feathers stuck together with wax.

Daedalus, who made the wings, was aware there could be problems if the wax got too hot, so warned his son to keep

By AL TITUDE,
Transport Correspondent

low. But once they were airborne Icarus got so excited he forgot the warning and glided higher and higher.

The increased heat from the sun's rays melted the wax. The feathers fell apart and Icarus plunged into the sea.

DROWNED

Last night he was missing, presumed drowned. Daedalus managed to land safely.

Last night a friend of Daedalus said: "He's obviously devas-

tated. He told the lad not to get too close to the sun. But you know what kids are like — in one ear and straight out of the other."

Icarus and Daedalus, a builder, made their flight in a desperate attempt to escape from the island of Crete.

They were being kept there against their will by the island's tyrannical King Minos. It is thought they were being held in a row over a palace extension which Daedalus built.

A spokesman for the king said last night: "His Majesty's thoughts are with Daedalus."

Fly Told You So — Pages 4 & 5

1327 BC

TUTANKHAMUN

THE tomb of the boy pharaoh Tutankhamun was discovered almost intact by British archaeologist Howard Carter in Egypt's Valley of the Kings in November 1922.

The gold coffins and fabulous treasures within stunned the world.

There were so many priceless items in the small tomb it took almost ten years to catalogue, remove and preserve them all.

But up until the find Tutankhamun was a little-known figure, with only a few references to him appearing in Egyptian documents.

Even today, the detail about much of his short life is far from certain, although there is evidence of an extensive building programme along with military expeditions against Nubia and Palestine.

Tutankhamun became Pharaoh in 1336BC on the death of his father Akhenaten. He was only nine years old, although married to his elder step-sister Ankhesenamun. His probable mother Kiya and his step-mother Nefertiti are both believed to have been dead by this date.

Egypt was therefore effectively ruled by the two most powerful men in the kingdom, a senior government official called Ay and an army leader called Horemheb.

Tutankhamun died in the ninth year of his reign, probably aged just 17.

Modern autopsies and X-rays show that he may have been killed by a fierce blow to the head, giving rise to the theory that he was murdered. Certainly Horemheb and Ay were the main beneficiaries of his death.

First, the ageing Ay became Pharaoh, taking Ankhesenamun as his queen to legitimise his rule.

Shortly afterwards her name disappears from the records.

Ay ruled for only four years. After his death Horemheb grabbed power. He tried to wipe out any record of Tutankhamun and Ay by substituting his name for theirs on monuments.

CARTER & THE CURSE

THE curse of Tutankhamun made headlines worldwide when Howard Carter's patron Lord Carnarvon died weeks after the tomb was opened.

Carnarvon, who funded Carter's expeditions, was killed by an infected mosquito bite.

But a story spread that he was the victim of a curse inscribed on the Pharaoh's tomb that claimed anyone who disturbed it would be "visited by wings of death."

No such inscription could ever be found. It was also reported that the lights went out in Cairo at the moment of Carnarvon's death in the city — while back in England his dog gave a terrible howl and died.

Further stories said Carter's pet canary was eaten by a cobra — one of the symbols of the Pharoah.

In following years more people linked to the tomb reportedly came to untimely ends, as recently as the 1990s.

Carter remained unharmed despite working in the tomb for ten years.

A wall painting of Pharaoh Tutankhamun and his wife

A highly-detailed perfume jar from the tomb of the Pharaoh

Howard Carter and a helper examine the sarcophagus of Pharaoh Tutankhamun in the Valley of the Kings near Luxor

...Timeline...

1333 Assyrians gain their independence from Babylon.

1330 Expansion of Hittite empire of Asia Minor.

An artist's impression of how Tutankhamun may have looked around the time of his death. Little is known about his short reign

Jewellery from the tomb. This piece has the emblems of the sun and moon

DON'T FORGET, IT'S MUMMY'S DAY

IT'S Mummy's Day tomorrow, folks — and you know she'll go embalmy if you forget tomb get her a present. So if you're looking for something yummy for your mummy, just turn to Page 23 for some great gift ideas

Murder of the boy king

PLOTTERS KILL TUTANKHAMUN

By NIALL CRUISE

BOY king Tutankhamun has been beaten to death in the grounds of his palace.

The 17-year-old Pharaoh's body was found late last night by a slave.

An examination revealed Tut had died from a massive blow to the head.

The Egyptian government last night claimed the Pharaoh may have suffered the injury tumbling out of his chariot during an evening drive.

But insiders at Tut's palace near the Nile insist the king was **MURDERED** as part of a plot to take over Egypt.

THRONE

One said: "It's no secret that there are some powerful men here who have had it in for the young king for quite a while."

The two chief suspects are the Egyptian army leader Horemheb and Tut's chief adviser Ay. Both are fiercely ambitious and have effectively run the country during the nine years Tut has been on the throne.

Insiders say they feared the king was preparing to take over the reins of power himself and force them into retirement.

Is Egypt Kaput Without Tut — Page 15

445,386 DAYS TO GO

A Bronze Age boat dating from 1300 — found by road builders in 1991. It is in the Dover Museum

...Timeline...

1300 Date of Bronze Age boat found during road building work in Dover, Kent, in 1991AD.

1275 Battle of Kadesh, Syria, between Egyptians, led by Pharaoh Ramesses II, and Hittites, ends in draw — they make peace.

1270 Scholar in Syria writes an encyclopedia.

1249 Temple of Ramesses II at Abu Simbel, southern Egypt, is built.

1230 Pharaoh Merneptah is at war with peoples of Israel.

1220 Troy, ancient city in north-western Anatolia (modern-day Turkey) destroyed by Myceneans after 10-year siege later described in Homer's Iliad (720BC).

A huge figure from the temple of Ramesses II in Abu Simbel, Egypt. It was constructed in 1249

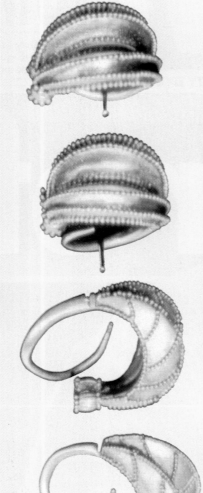

Gold earrings, necklaces and a head decoration found by archaeologists who discovered the ruins of Troy

1220BC

THE TROJAN WAR

The ruins of the walls of Troy at the modern-day Turkish town of Hissarlik. Experts who worked on the site say the ancient city was destroyed by fire

THE Trojan War is perhaps the most famous of all Greek legends. It tells of the ten-year siege of the city of Troy (in Anatolia in modern-day Turkey) and the eventual destruction of that city by a Greek army led by King Agamemnon.

The war broke out after Paris, son of Trojan king Priam, ran off with the beautiful Helen, wife of Menelaus, ruler of Sparta in southern Greece.

The lovers returned to Troy, but Menelaus could not allow such a terrible insult to go unavenged. A vast army was collected under the command of his brother Agamemnon.

The troops were loaded on to 1,000 ships which set off for Troy. Agamemnon's army contained many famous warriors, like Odysseus, Ajax and the famous fighter Achilles — who could only be killed if he was wounded in the heel.

The first nine years of the siege were largely uneventful, but in the tenth the hot-tempered Achilles withdrew from the fighting following a row with Agamemnon.

His withdrawal inspired the Trojans, led by Priam's eldest son Hector, who burst from the city and inflicted a series of defeats on the Greeks.

Achilles' beloved friend Patroclus realised that the demoralised Greeks were facing certain defeat without their hero to inspire them.

So he persuaded the sulking Achilles to lend him his armour, hoping it would fool the Trojans into thinking Achilles had returned to the fight. The ruse failed to work and Patroclus was killed by Hector.

The grief-stricken Achilles now returned to the fighting for real and killed Hector.

Achilles himself was later killed after he was hit in the heel by an arrow fired by Paris — and guided to its spot by the god Apollo. Troy was finally taken by a clever trick. The Greeks built a huge wooden horse, inside which a few hand-picked warriors were hidden.

The rest of the army then boarded their ships and pretended to sail away, leaving the wooden horse outside the gates of Troy as a peace offering.

Most of the Trojans were completely fooled. Only the priest Laocoon sensed something was wrong. He warned his fellow citizens not to take the gift inside the city walls.

But as Laocoon spoke two giant snakes slithered from the sea and killed him and his two sons. The snakes were sent by the goddess Athena, who supported the Greeks.

Her plan worked. The Trojans believed the killing of Laocoon proved the gods would be offended if they did not accept the gift and they dragged it within the city walls.

As soon as darkness fell, the Greeks emerged from the horse and opened the gates of the city.

The rest of the Greek army, which had silently returned, flooded in. The city was sacked and burned. Its inhabitants were either killed or sold into slavery. Only a handful escaped.

The story of the climax of the Trojan War is told in an epic poem called the Iliad.

It is thought to have been written around 800BC by a blind poet known to us as Homer, and is widely accepted as the beginning of European literature.

A sequel to the events at Troy, called The Odyssey, is also believed to have been written by Homer. It tells of how the hero Odysseus made his way home to Greece.

The Trojan War itself is traditionally dated to the 12th Century BC.

Modern archaeological excavations at the site of ancient Troy (Hissarlik in Turkey) have shown it was destroyed by fire in the early part of the era.

THE Sun

hursday, October 2, 1220BC   THOUGHT: TROY STORY

HORSE DUPE SENSATION

Crafty Greeks capture Troy by hiding in wooden pony

EXCLUSIVE

By HEIDI HOLE

THE ten-year siege of Troy is over — after the daft Trojans were conned by a giant horse made of WOOD.

The crafty Greek attackers got their carpenters to knock up the horse, then hid a few warriors in its hollow interior.

The Greek army pretended to go home, leaving the horse outside Troy's walls as a peace offering.

The dopey Trojans believed the enemy had given up, opened their gates and dragged the horse inside.

When it was dark the Greeks climbed from the nag and opened the gates for their pals, who were hiding nearby.

SLITHERED

The army stormed in as the Trojans slept and easily took control of the city.

A priest who warned the Trojans not to take the wooden horse into the city was mysteriously killed by two giant snakes, it was revealed last night.

Laocoon suspected that the Greeks were playing a trick and begged his fellow citizens not to open the city gates.

But as he was speaking two giant snakes slithered out of the nearby sea and choked the priest to death.

His two sons, who went to his aid, were also killed. It is believed that one of the gods may have been behind the slayings.

A Trojan police spokesman said last night: "I can only tell you that we are currently treating the deaths as suspicious."

Helen Of Joy — Pages 4 and 5

Deadly . . . snakes attack the priest

Wood you believe it . . . the giant timber horse used to capture Troy. Somehow the Trojans failed to spot the windows in the side

1200 BC

STORY OF MOSES

MOSES is revered as the greatest of the Old Testament prophets — the man who delivered the Israelites from slavery.

The book of Exodus tells how the Hebrews were living in bondage under the Egyptian Pharaoh at the time of Moses's birth.

The Pharaoh wanted to control the Hebrew population, so ordered that all baby boys be put to death.

But Moses's parents avoided the order by putting him in a basket of reeds and setting it afloat on the Nile.

The tot was found by the Pharaoh's daughter, who rescued him.

In the following years, Moses was raised at Pharaoh's court, where he was educated as a prince.

As he grew he learned he was a Hebrew and became curious to know more of his people. So he decided to visit them — and was horrified to find them living as slaves.

He was so appalled to see one Hebrew being beaten by his Egyptian foreman that he killed the brute. The next day he returned, determined to help the Hebrews. But when he intervened in a row between two of them they turned on him.

One said: "Are you going to kill me, like you did that Egyptian?"

Moses realised the Pharaoh would hear of what he had done and so decided to flee to northern Arabia.

He settled there among a people called the Midianites.

One day, while he was looking after some sheep, he came across a bush that was burning.

Suddenly a voice warned Moses to come no closer and told him he was standing on holy ground.

According to the Old Testament, Moses realised he was being spoken to by God — who ordered him to bring the Hebrews out of Egypt.

Moses was reluctant, but eventually agreed. Egypt was ruled at the time by the Pharaoh Ramesses II. Moses confronted him and explained his mission from God.

But Ramesses, who was used to being treated as a god himself, refused to free the Hebrews.

Moses despaired of being able to persuade the Pharaoh, but God vowed to send a series of plagues designed to force Ramesses's hand.

First the River Nile was turned into blood. Then the country was plagued by frogs, flies, mosquitos, cattle disease, boils, storms, locusts and thick darkness.

Grudgingly, Ramesses acknowledged the power of Moses's God, but still refused to free the Hebrews. Finally God demonstrated his power by killing the eldest children all the people of Egypt — apart from the Hebrews.

Ramesses's own son was among the dead. He was so shaken he ordered the Hebrews to leave Egypt.

But he soon changed his mind and sent his army after them. The soldiers cornered them at the shores of the Sea of Reeds, usually interpreted as the Red Sea.

Moses called on God for help. A wind blew up, causing the sea to part and creating a dry channel through which the Hebrews passed.

The Egyptians pursued, but were killed when the waters flooded back.

Moses led the Hebrews on to Mount Sinai. Here, God gave him tablets of stone on which were carved the Ten Commandments — the rules which God now expected the Hebrews to obey.

The Hebrews wandered in the wilderness for 40 years as they sought the Promised Land.

Finally they reached its borders. According to the Bible, an aged Moses climbed a mountain so he could look down over this longed-for territory.

The Old Testament says the Hebrews never saw him again. There is no mention of how he died.

Moses hears the voice of the Lord from within the burning bush (left) telling him to return to Egypt and rescue the Hebrews from slavery. Right, Pharaoh's daughter returns to her father's palace with her servants after finding baby Moses floating on the River Nile in a basket made of reeds. Both paintings are from the 19th century

A wall carving showing the Egyptians battling the Sea Peoples, who invaded around 1200

...Timeline...

1200 Assyrians make their first menacing appearance in Middle East; Celts dominate central Europe; Israelites leave Egypt for Palestine; Egypt and coastal regions of Palestine and Asia Minor invaded by migrating tribes known as the Sea Peoples. In Britain, warriors begin to take a central role in society; Improvement in farming in southern England sees farms consisting of groups of small circular huts, small rectangular fields and enclosures for the raising of livestock.

A wall carving from the temple of the Pharaoh Ramesses III shows him fighting the Sea Peoples

GM CROPS SCANDAL

By MO MEADOW

ANGRY protesters are calling on British farmers to stop their experiments with geographically-modified crops.

They say the new trend of fencing off enclosed areas — called fields — for the growing of crops could be damaging to our health. A spokesman for MAFF, Men Against Foolish Farming, said: "We are interfering with nature by experimenting with this GM farming. It is immoral.

"Plants and crops are meant to grow wild and free — not be crowded in together in these hideous prisons that they call fields."

GM Food Turned My Head Green — Page 9

FREED BY A MIRACLE

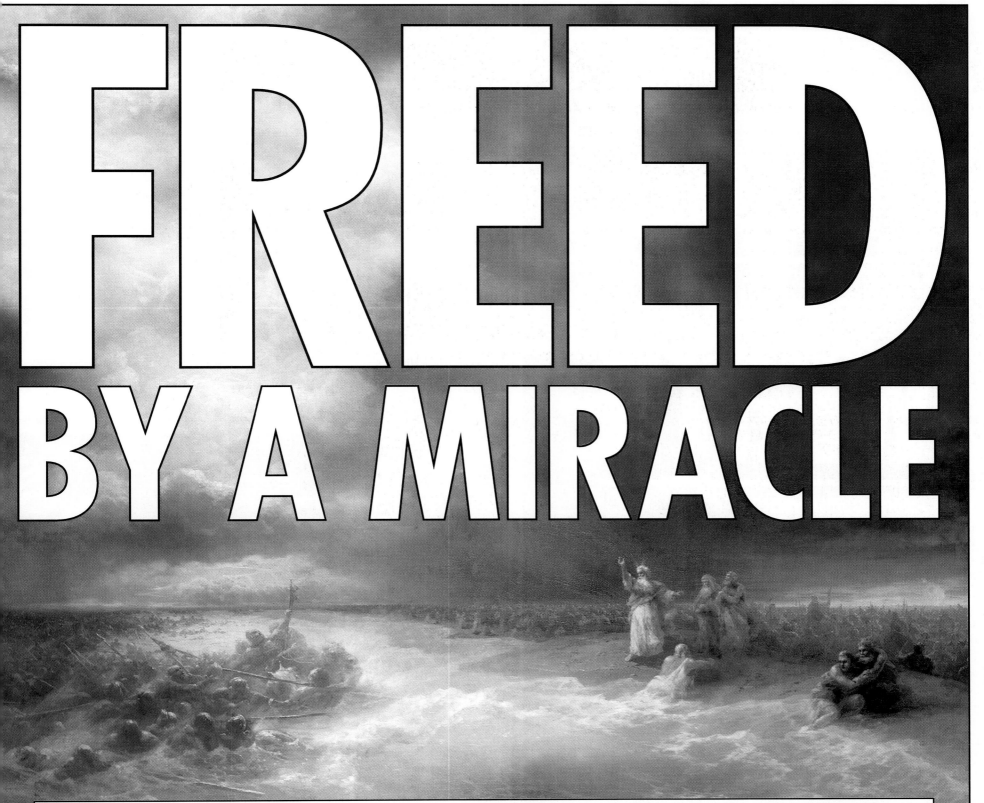

Moses gets Hebrews out

From DEN COMMANDMENTS
on the shores of the Red Sea

MAGNIFICENT Moses managed to sneak the runaway Hebrews out of Egypt last night — after persuading God to send them a miracle in a million.

The Hebrews, fleeing after generations of slavery, were cornered by the Pharaoh's army on the edge of the Red Sea.

But their leader begged God for help — and He sent a vast wind that **PARTED** the sea so the Hebrews could cross.

The stunned Egyptian soldiers could not believe their eyes, but decided to try to follow in their chariots.

When they were half-way across, the wind suddenly dropped. The sea surged back into the gap, drowning the entire Egyptian army.

Last night officials in the Egyptian government were trying to cover up the disaster. The Pharaoh's official press spokesman even denied that the army had been destroyed.

He said: "The troops are fine. They are currently on manoeuvres in the Red Sea region. After that they are due for a spell of extended leave."

Moses was last night believed to be leading the Hebrews in the direction of Mount Sinai. He hopes to found an independent Hebrew state somewhere in the Middle East — with the provisional title of The Promised Land.

Insiders say he already has plans for a detailed series of laws designed to keep the notoriously quarrelsome Hebrews from going off the rails.

But sources close to Moses last night said it was impossible to put a timescale on his dream of founding a state.

One said: "All I can say is that we hope to have it up and running as soon as possible. After all, we don't want to be wandering around here for the next 40 years."

Victims Of God's Wrath — Pages 4 and 5

Victims of God's wrath

Arrogant . . . Ramesses II thought he was more powerful than God

PLAGUES

From MAL TREATMENT
on the banks of the Nile

EGYPT'S mighty ruler Ramesses II has seen his land ravaged with a series of terrible plagues — because he stupidly tried to stop God getting his own way.

The Pharaoh sparked God's wrath when he snubbed a plea from Moses that the Hebrews be released from slavery.

Instead, he arrogantly challenged Moses to prove that the Hebrew God was more powerful than him — the ruler of an Egyptian empire with an army of 600 chariots.

God responded in devastating style — sending epidemics of blood, frogs, dead cows, mosquitos, flies, boils, locusts and storms.

Then, to hammer home the point, he killed the first-born of **EVERY** non-Hebrew family in Egypt. Ramesses' son was among those who perished.

Last night a royal insider said: "Ramesses must have been mad to take on God.

Sarcastic

"He is the greatest ruler we have ever had, but the wealth and power must have gone to his head."

The war of words between Moses — God's 80-year-old spokesman — and Ramesses will probably go down as one of the great head-to-heads of history.

It began when Moses, accompanied by his 83-year-old brother Aaron, marched into Ramesses' palace and asked to have a quiet word.

When the Pharaoh agreed to see them, Moses got straight to the point, saying: "The God of Israel wants you to let his people, the Hebrews, go free so they can worship him in peace."

Ramesses, who has had thousands of Hebrews working for him in appalling conditions, replied: "Who does this God think he is, ordering me about? Get out!"

After Moses and Aaron had gone, Ramesses decided to teach them a lesson.

He ordered his slavemasters to make the Hebrews work ever harder, sending a sarcastic message, which read. "Clearly the Hebrews have too much time on their hands and that's why they are grumbling."

Contempt

When the Hebrew spokesman complained about the extra work, Pharaoh simply shrugged and said: "Blame your pal Moses."

His ploy had the desired effect of turning the Hebrew workmen against Moses.

He began to despair, but God urged him to keep trying. Moses decided he would have to prove just how powerful God was.

So he arranged another meeting with the Pharaoh and showed off his powers. He hurled a stick on the floor and it became a snake.

Ramesses was not impressed. He called in his court magicians who repeated the trick.

Moses's serpent swallowed the magicians' one, but Pharaoh waved him away.

He said with contempt: "You have failed to prove your God is more powerful." Pharaoh's attitude infuriated God, who decided to show him who was boss once and for all. So over the next few months he struck Egypt with a series of horrific plagues.

First was the **RIVER OF BLOOD.** This involved God turning the Nile water into blood, killing all the fish. The stench was appalling. Even worse, it caused a huge shortage in water for drinking and irrigating crops.

Second came a plague of **FROGS.** The slimy creatures invaded the homes of Egyptians in their hundreds. People would often find up to 20 in their bathroom. And the noise they made was unbearable, croaking through the night and ruining people's sleep.

Next came vast clouds of **MOSQUITOS,** making life a nightmare with their constant bit-

ing. Pharaoh's magicians were by now getting scared. One told Ramesses: "This is the work of God." But Pharaoh refused to budge.

After the mosquitos came another insect horror – swarms of **FLIES.** The creepy-crawlies got everywhere – but miraculously the Hebrews were unaffected.

Weaken

By now, Pharaoh's resolve was beginning to weaken. But he did not want to appear to back down so he offered a compromise.

He told Moses he would allow the Hebrews to go off and worship their God in peace – as long as they stayed within the borders of Egypt.

Moses refused, saying God

The River Nile turned from water to blood, killing all the fish

Swarms of nasty gnats had pharaoh's magicians running scared

Locusts ate everything in their path — and ruined the economy

FROGS

Slimy frogs drove everyone round the bend — getting under people's feet and croaking day and night

FLIES

Pharaoh began to waver when his lands were invaded by flies

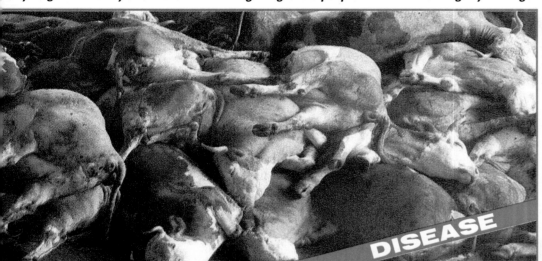

DISEASE

Pestilence killed off entire herds of cattle belonging to Egyptians. But Hebrew cows were unharmed

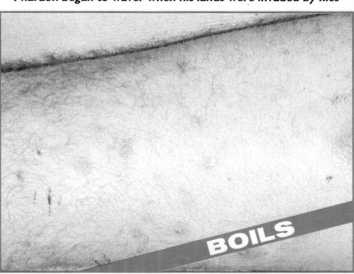

BOILS

Moses produced a vast dust cloud that left behind a plague of boils

STORMS

Egypt was devastated by a series of violent storms that brought torrents of rain, hail and thunder

SLAUGHTER

Final affliction led to death of the first-born of all non-Hebrews

had commanded them to venture three days' journey into the wilderness beyond Egypt's borders.

Meanwhile, the plagues continued. Next was a **DISEASE** that killed all the Egyptians' cattle, ruining many farmers. Again, the few cows owned by the Hebrews were unharmed.

Moses then produced a spectacular trick. While standing in front of Pharaoh he tossed a handful of dust into the air.

The dust grew into a huge cloud that spread over the land. When it fell to earth and touched the skin of either men or animals it immediately left a rash of painful **BOILS**.

The magicians were so afflicted by the boils that they could not attend any of the

meetings between Ramesses and Moses. Next came a series of terrible **STORMS,** with hail, rain, thunder and lightning.

Ramesses now seemed to have had enough. He told Moses: "OK. I realise I was wrong. You can take the Hebrews away."

But as soon as the storms stopped, he changed his mind. Moses warned that there would be a new plague — of **LOCUSTS**.

Famine

So the Pharaoh tried another compromise. He offered to let the Hebrew men go out of the country to worship — but insisted on keeping the women and children to ensure their return.

Moses turned the offer down

— and within days millions of locusts came flying into Egypt in huge clouds. The tiny insects were not just an irritation — they devastated the economy by eating all the crops and every other plant in their path.

Pharaoh realised that without crops the country was staring famine in the face.

He urgently summoned Moses and Aaron and said: "I may have been a little hasty in rejecting your plea.

"Please ask your God to remove the locusts and the matter of the Hebrews will be sorted out instantly."

God called off the locusts — and once again Ramesses broke his word. Moses tried one more bit of gentle persuasion, calling in a great dark cloud that blot-

ted out all sunshine for three days. But it was hopeless. Pharaoh not only refused to budge, but threatened to kill Moses if he saw his face again.

So God decided to send his most awesome punishment — the **KILLING OF THE FIRST-BORN**.

Each Hebrew family was told to kill a lamb and daub its blood over the top of their front doors in the shape of a cross.

Grim

Moses also told them to pack their things, because God was about to lead them from captivity in Egypt.

A few hours later all the first-born across the land were mysteriously struck down by the angel of the Lord. Only the houses that displayed the sign

of blood were spared — the angel passing over these as he flew around carrying out his grim task.

Pharaoh, whose own son perished, was inconsolable.

He begged Moses to take the Hebrews from the country — and even gave them gold, silver and clothes as parting gifts.

But just a few days after the Hebrews had gone Pharaoh decided he wanted revenge.

He summoned his massive army and sent if after the unarmed Hebrews. The insider said: "It was a crazy decision — he just didn't seem to think it through."

The Egyptian chariots finally caught up with the Hebrews yesterday at the Red Sea.

And once again God taught arrogant Pharaoh a lesson he will never forget.

397,874 DAYS TO GO

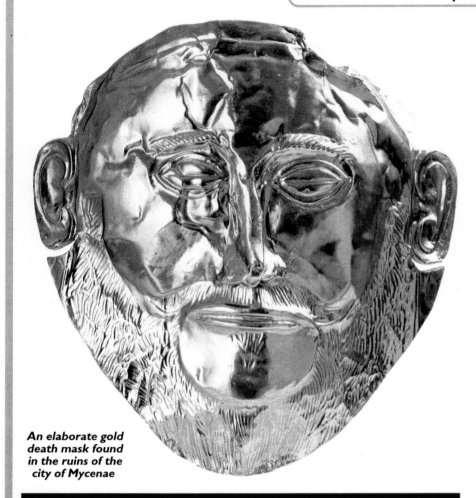

An elaborate gold death mask found in the ruins of the city of Mycenae

...Timeline...

1180 Phrygians, from west-central Anatolia, invade Asia Minor.

1177 Sea Peoples driven back by Egypt.

1151 Egypt's last great Pharaoh, Ramesses III, dies.

1150 Destruction of city of Mycenae in Southern Greece.

1122 Start of the reign of the Zhou Dynasty in China.

1111 Egyptians investigate wide-scale tomb robbery in the Valley of Kings.

1100 Date of earliest hilltop forts in western Europe; Phoenicians, from what is now the Lebanon, spread throughout Mediterranean and develop alphabetic script, basis of European languages today; Onset of a 300-year Dark Age in Greece in which civilisation effectively breaks down; Britain's population thought to have hit one million around this time.

The Lion Gate at the ruins of the ancient city of Mycenae in Southern Greece, which was destroyed around 1150. Right, armour worn by Mycenean warriors

1100 BC

SAMSON & DELILAH

THE story of how Samson was betrayed by his lover Delilah is one of the best-loved Bible stories. The Old Testament tells how before Samson was born an angel told his mother that he was destined to begin to deliver the Israelites from their oppressors, the Philistines.

But the angel warned that on no account should his hair ever be cut.

Samson grew to be a man of immense strength and after a series of rows with the Philistines, waged war on them — at one stage killing 1,000, even though he was only armed with the jawbone of an ass.

Finally, the Philistines decided to ensnare Samson using his well-known fondness for attractive women.

They enlisted the help of Delilah, promising her a fortune if she found the secret of Samson's strength.

Samson soon fell for Delilah and the pair became lovers.

After a few days she asked him if it was possible for his great strength to be overcome.

He told her a lie, saying that if he was bound with seven bowstrings he would be as weak as any ordinary man.

She duly tied him up, but when she shouted "The Philistines are here!" he swiftly broke free.

Delilah tried to discover his secret on two more occasions.

Both times he told a lie. She refused to give up and asked him every day, until fed-up Samson admitted his uncut hair was the secret of his superhuman strength.

While Samson slept, Delilah shaved his hair, then called in the Philistines. He awoke as they grabbed him, but was too weak to resist.

The Philistines gouged his eyes out and jailed him — but forgot to ensure his hair was kept trimmed.

One day, after it had grown back, they brought him into one of their crowded temples to torment him.

They tied him to the pillars, but the rejuvenated Samson pulled them down, bringing the temple roof crashing in.

The Bible says more than 3,000 were killed, including Samson.

A blinded Samson uses his superhuman strength to pull down the stone pillars of the Philistine temple, killing himself and his enemies

BOOMING BRITAIN

ARCHAEOLOGISTS believe that Britain's population probably hit one million before the beginning of the first millennium BC.

It coincided with the building of the first hillforts and the increasingly sophisticated manufacture of gold and bronze items.

Over the next 500 years a series of improvements in farming techniques allowed the production of greater numbers of crops.

This in turn supported a further growth in population, which reached about 1.5million by 500BC.

By the beginning of the Christian era Britain's population may have soared to as much as four million. Julius Caesar, in his writings on Britain, said: "The population is extremely large."

THE Sun

Tuesday, December 6, 1090BC

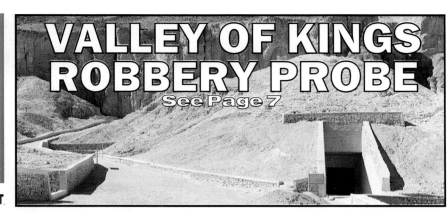

1M

Crowding alert over Britain's sky-high population

By TERRY BULCRUSH

BRITAIN'S population has reached a staggering **ONE MILLION,** says a new study.

Boffins say improvements in our food quality have helped boost the birth rate.

And they reckon the population could swell by half again in the next 500 years if the trend goes on.

But they warn that the island may become horribly overcrowded unless we act soon.

More new villages will have to be built — and existing settlements will have to be expanded.

Smell

Environment groups last night said the news was "extremely grim."

A spokesman for Keep Britain Backward said: "We foresee a time when there will be as many as five families living in one village.

"The overcrowding, noise and smell will be an absolute nightmare."

The study came up with the population figure by taking the average number of people in a village and multiplying it by a big number.

Hut prices go through the thatch
PAGES 20 & 21

WHY, WHY, WHY, DELILAH

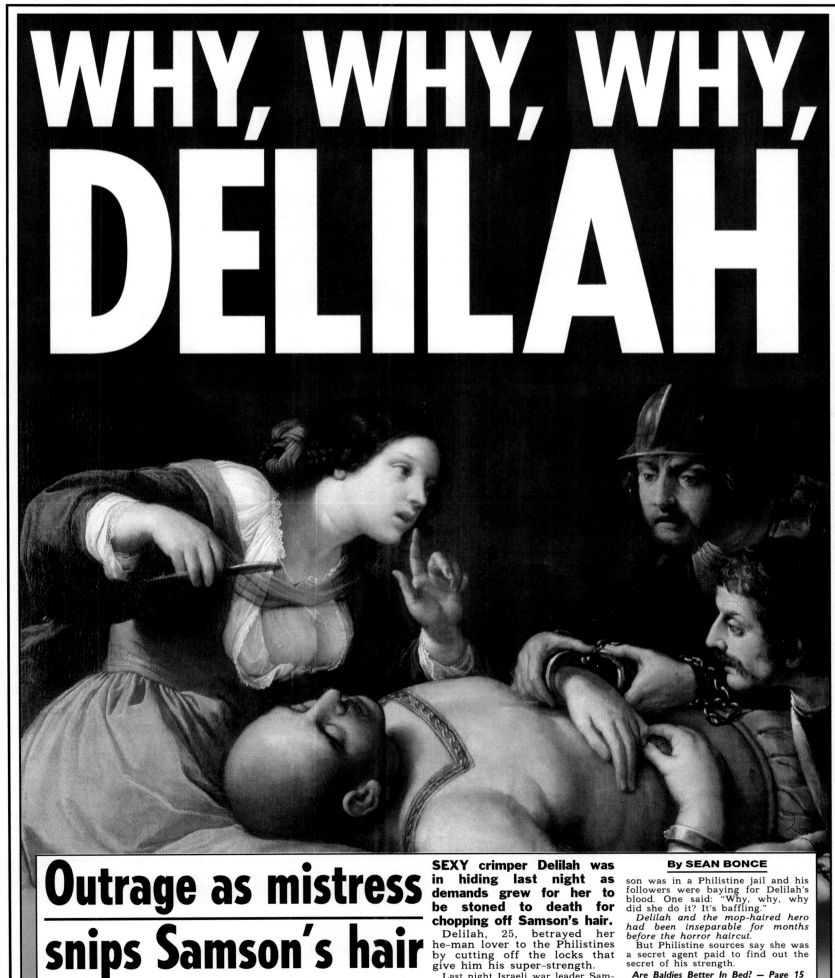

Outrage as mistress snips Samson's hair

SEXY crimper Delilah was in hiding last night as demands grew for her to be stoned to death for chopping off Samson's hair.

Delilah, 25, betrayed her he-man lover to the Philistines by cutting off the locks that give him his super-strength.

Last night Israeli war leader Sam-

By SEAN BONCE

son was in a Philistine jail and his followers were baying for Delilah's blood. One said: "Why, why, why did she do it? It's baffling."

Delilah and the mop-haired hero had been inseparable for months before the horror haircut.

But Philistine sources say she was a secret agent paid to find out the secret of his strength.

Are Baldies Better In Bed? — Page 15

374,392 DAYS TO GO

1025 BC

KING DAVID

THE story of David — the shepherd boy who became Israel's king — is one of the greatest of the Old Testament tales.

The Bible tells how his rise to supreme power effectively began when he killed the giant Goliath, champion of the hated Philistines, in single combat.

After this he was summoned to the court of the Israelite king Saul to be the monarch's official armour carrier.

David was also a skilled musician and his harp-playing was said to be able to cure the king's fits of rage. As David grew older his military abilities came to the fore and he was soon winning fame for his daring campaigns against the Philistines.

He also became firm friends with Jonathan, Saul's son and heir.

But David's success and popularity began to alarm Saul, who saw him as a dangerous rival.

Saul eventually decided to kill David and openly waged war against him. But after both Saul and Jonathan were killed in a disastrous battle against the Philistines, David filled the political vacuum and become king of the Israelites.

David made Jerusalem his capital and set about consolidating his rule. Once he was secure, he used his excellent army to defeat neighbouring enemies like the Philistines, Moabites, Aramaeans and Edomites. These victories allowed him to expand his kingdom to the north, east and south. It was during one of these campaigns that David famously committed adultery with the beautiful Bathsheba.

When she fell pregnant he deliberately sent her husband Uriah to his death by ordering him to fight in the front line.

Shortly afterwards, David's son Absolom tried to seize power but was killed as the rebellion was crushed. David was succeeded by Solomon, his son by Bathsheba.

Medieval paintings and engravings showing scenes from the life of King David. Left and centre, he is seen with his harp. Right, David is pictured killing Goliath and in attendance at the court of Saul

HILL CARVINGS

THE White Horse at Uffington, Oxfordshire, is the oldest and most famous of the ancient figures carved into Britain's chalk hills, though Dorset's Cerne Abbas giant is also memorable.

Recent excavations have dated the 374ft long horse at around 1000BC. It is now believed it was the inspiration for a series of other hill carvings.

Its purpose is not known. One theory is that it represents the Celtic horse goddess Epona and was a site for worship.

Dragon Hill, next to it, is where St George slayed the dragon, according to much later legend.

Uffington's White Horse inspired many hill carvings. They include the one above at Westbury, Wilts, which was cut in 1778, though locals insist an original version on the hill was far older

...Timeline...

1027 Start of the reign of the Western Zhou dynasty in China.

1025 King David transforms Hebrews into formidable empire (it splits up under his successors); Assyrians ascend to dominance of the Middle East thanks to powerful chariot-based army.

THE Sun

Wednesday, April 27, 1025BC

THOUGHT: FOAL PLAY

MORONS
Outrage as graffiti
gang deface hillside

By LAURA NORDER,
Crime Correspondent

VANDALS have caused fury by gouging a hideous horse shape in the side of a chalk hill.

The site is a mecca for families who like to climb up to enjoy meat-based picnics while gazing out over miles of beautiful countryside.

Now their view will be blighted by the sickening 374ft-long eyesore.

The graffiti, pictured left, is so large that birds probably have the best view of it.

Louts

Rural campaigners fear the horse, a few dozen miles from Stonehenge, will spark a wave of copycat attacks on other beauty spots.

One said: "This may be only the beginning. We fear this kind of graffiti could spring up everywhere.

"The country is so sparsely populated that louts could spend weeks doing one of these and no one would ever spot them.

"The problem is that these lads are bored and have nowhere else to go.

"Add to that the fact there is no police force and pretty much no law and order at all and you've got a recipe for disaster."

Hoofdunnit — Page 9

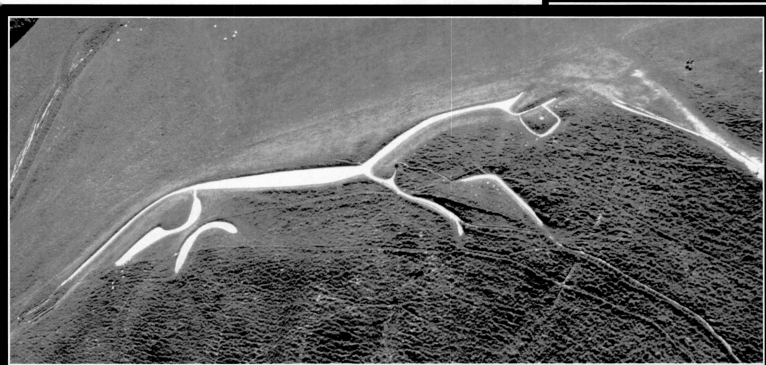

BIG FIGHT SENSATION
GIANT KILLER
Diddy David KO's
Goliath the great

Heads I win . . . David decapitates Goliath as the fight ends

By DEE CAPITATE

THE fight world was reeling last night after no-hoper David KO'd legendary brawler Goliath in the greatest giant-killing ever.

He poleaxed the Philistine brute just seconds into the bout by hurling a stone at his head.

The pebble smashed into its target

EXCLUSIVE

and Goliath — almost 9ft tall and weighing close to 30 stone — hit the deck with a deafening thud.

Before Goliath could be counted out the featherweight Hebrew hero, who is only a shade over 5ft 4ins, leapt forward and chopped off his head to make victory certain.

Amazingly, minutes earlier David's friends had been urging him to pull

out of the fight because his opponent was deemed unbeatable. On paper it certainly looked as if only a mug punter would back the 1,000-1 outsider against the odds-on favourite.

Goliath — dubbed the Beast from the Middle East — had never lost a fight, winning most of his contests with ferocious knockouts.

In contrast David, a full-time shepherd, had only the experience of a few small bouts against wolves who attacked his flock.

1000-1 SHOT GIVES BOOKIES A CANING
FULL STORY OF AN AMAZING UPSET — SEE BACK PAGE

346,904 DAYS TO GO

950BC

KING SOLOMON

SOLOMON is more famous today for his reputation for wisdom than for his achievements as King of Israel — and the greatest example is the Biblical account of how he settled the dispute over the baby.

What we know of Solomon is, in fact, almost entirely down to the descriptions in the Old Testament books of Kings and Chronicles — fact-packed works which scholars believe to be highly reliable.

Solomon was the son of King David and wife Bathsheba. He took the throne in 961BC on David's death and quickly wiped out his enemies and put friends in power.

He then set about establishing Israel as a huge commercial empire. Solomon made trade deals with other kings and kept them sweet by adding a vast number of their sisters and daughters to his harem. The

Bible says he had 700 wives, though this is unlikely, even for a man noted for excess.

Solomon maintained the stability of his empire with huge military force. He also made slaves out of the Canaanites whose cities had long ago been conquered by Israel.

The Queen of nearby Sheba came to see Israel's prosperity for herself — in one of the two episodes for which Solomon is most famous.

Her wealthy kingdom in south Arabia lay between Israel and the Indian Ocean, which Solomon needed access to in order to trade overseas in the east.

Meanwhile Solomon had control of ports in Palestine, which allowed him to trade in the Mediterranean, and the Queen wanted him to market her goods in that direction. The lavish arrival of the Queen of Sheba has

been portrayed in books and films. It is described in 2 Chronicles 9 as "a very great retinue and camels bearing spices and very much gold and precious stones." Legend has it that the two became lovers and even had a child.

In Jerusalem Solomon built a city wall, a palace and his greatest single achievement, the first Temple, completed around 957BC. Hundreds of years later the site, though not the building itself, became the focal point for early Christians.

The baby dispute is described in 1 Kings 3, Verses 16-28.

It tells how two women, each claiming to be the mother of the same baby, approach the King asking him to settle the dispute.

Solomon tells them to cut the baby in half and share it — knowing that its real mother will rather give the

child to the other woman than see it killed. The bogus mother, however — in reality grief-stricken over the death of her own baby — would rather see the living child killed than give it up.

Solomon is also said to have been a great writer, with all sorts of works attributed to him, many wrongly. They include the Proverbs, the Song of Solomon, Ecclesiastes, the Wisdom of Solomon, the Psalms of Solomon and the Odes of Solomon.

Wise he may have been, but Solomon left a fragile empire which self-destructed after his death in 922BC. It is thought that because of his personal excesses, Israel's great wealth did not filter down to the ordinary people, for whom he had little time.

And Solomon's dismissive treatment of tribes in the north resulted in them splitting the empire in two.

'The Queen Of Sheba Before King Solomon' by 18th Century painter Giambattista Tiepolo. Their meeting, described in the Bible, has since been portrayed in film, art and literature

Dying King David hands sceptre of power to Solomon in this 17th Century work by Cornelis de Vos. Solomon built Israel up, but disregarded his people

CHINESE INVENTIONS

THE ancient Chinese were among the most inventive peoples of all time. Among the many things they can claim to have introduced in the thousand years before Christ are the bell, an early form of plastic, the iron plough, kites, umbrellas and a primitive compass.

Many everyday items we now take for granted were invented

in China hundreds or even thousands of years before they reached the West.

For example, the Chinese began to use paper sometime around 200BC — about 1,400 years before it came to Europe.

They are even thought to have developed an early type of chemical warfare, using poisonous gas against their

enemies some 2,300 years before its use during World War One.

Some of their ideas failed to catch on. Around 1200BC they began using sea shells as money. They were later replaced in some areas by money made of leather — with 1ft square pieces of deerskin used to represent large denominations.

...Timeline...

1000 Umbrella and kite both invented in China; Phoenician trade begins in Mediterranean.

965 Solomon, known as the Wise, becomes king of Israel.

957 Solomon builds first Temple in Jerusalem to house the Ark of the Covenant.

Brilliant . . . the 'rainbattler'

Chinese invent a device to keep rain off head

From **SONNY OUTLOOK** in China

INGENIOUS inventors in China have solved the age-old problem of how to keep your head dry when it rains.

They have come up with a device shaped like an upturned dish which is held over the head on a stick.

When the rain hits the dish-shaped area — which can be made of wood, thatch or fabric — it rolls down the sides.

The device, called a rainbattler, allows people to take a stroll in any weather without fear of a soaking.

The Chinese have also

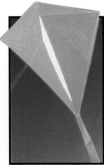

Kite . . . wind-powered

recently invented a flying machine called a kite. The kites, which come in many shapes, colours and sizes, are made of a lightweight fabric stretched over a wooden frame.

When a strong wind blows, currents catch in the kite's fabric and carry it into the air.

Kite-users usually tie a rope to one end of their machine — otherwise reclaiming it once the wind has dropped can be very time-consuming.

Neither the rainbattler nor the kite will be available in Britain for years.

IS THAT WISE SOLOMON?

We're all a bit throne . . . women wail after Solomon demands sword and suggests slicing baby in half to settle dispute yesterday

King says: Cut tug-of-love baby in half

KING Solomon's wisdom was under fire last night after he suggested that a tug-of-love baby should be CUT IN HALF.

The crazy ruling was greeted with outrage by child protection groups.

Even his closest advisers were astonished. One senior aide told The Sun: "He must have gone mad." The Israeli King's lunatic

By ARTHUR KIDD

decision came after two women asked him to settle their dispute over which was the kid's mum.

Solomon's reputation for wisdom is legendary.

But he stunned the women and his own courtiers when he demanded that a sword be brought to him.

Then he said the feuding pair should share the tot by having half each.

One woman was distraught

and screamed at the idea of killing the baby, even offering to give up her custody battle.

But her cold-hearted rival has accepted the baby's slaughter in principle.

Solomon will make his judgement tomorrow.

His aide said: "We can't believe he's serious about killing this child. It must be some sort of ruse.

"We hope he gets a good night's sleep. This would be a bad one to get wrong."

The case continues.

295,986 DAYS TO GO

810 BC

THE MIDAS TOUCH

King Midas turns his roses into gold in a 19th century engraving. The Midas story is a classic Greek myth of how one man's greed almost ruined his life

THE story of King Midas and his ability to turn everything he touched to gold is one of the most famous fables of all time — a classic myth telling of the tragedy that befalls those who have everything but still want more.

Midas is said to have lived and ruled in Phrygia, in modern Turkey. According to the legend, he had everything a ruler could want — a beautiful land, a huge fortune and a lovely daughter named Zoe whom he loved dearly.

But what he loved most was gold . . . amassing a huge collection of gold coins and decorating his palace with gold trinkets.

One day Dionysus, the god of wine, was passing through Midas's territory when one of his friends became lost. Midas looked after the man and later made sure he was reunited with Dionysus. The god was so grateful he offered to grant Midas one wish.

Midas immediately said: "I want everything I touch to turn to gold."

Dionysus was reluctant to grant the wish, but agreed when Midas insisted there was nothing else he wanted.

The god left after telling Midas that when he awoke the next morning his wish would have been fulfilled.

When Midas woke the next day he reached out to touch his bedside table . . . and it turned to gold.

He was so excited he leapt from bed and ran around his palace, touching one item after another . . . and turning them all into gold.

After a couple of hours he realised he was hungry and went to his banqueting hall for breakfast. As he sat down he grabbed a rose and tried to put it to his nose to smell its fragrance, but it immediately turned to gold.

He frowned and picked up a grape and popped it in his mouth . . . and nearly broke a tooth as he chomped down on the golden ball. Next he tried to eat a piece of bread and drink a glass of wine, but both turned to gold at his touch.

Midas, realising suddenly how stupid he had been, broke down and cried.

His daughter Zoe heard her father's sobs and ran to see what was wrong. Before he could stop her she leapt into his arms to comfort him . . . and turned into a golden statue.

Heartbroken Midas prayed to Dionysus for aid, begging him: "Please take this curse away from me." The god took pity on Midas, telling him he would restore Zoe and the other items to their previous state — on the condition that Midas gave up all the gold in his kingdom. The king readily agreed.

When his daughter was returned to him, Midas was so pleased he gave away the rest of his possessions and moved to a small cabin on the edge of a forest.

Midas is also the central character in another Greek myth.

According to this legend he was asked to judge a musical contest between the gods Apollo, who played a stringed instrument called a lyre, and Pan, who played his musical pipes.

Midas picked Pan — a decision that so enraged Apollo that he turned Midas's ears in those of a donkey. The king was forced to wear a hat for the rest of his life to stop his subjects discovering how ridiculous he looked.

...Timeline..

924 Pharaoh Shoshenk I invades Palestine.

922 Solomon dies, son Rehoboam takes over; Hebrew kingdom divided in two, the northern area becomes Israel, the southern Judah.

900 China has a postal service.

859 Shalmeneser III becomes king of Assyria — Israel pays homage to him.

814 North African city of Carthage founded by traders from city of Tyre, Phoenicia — Carthaginians become the Western Mediterranean's dominant economic power.

Decorations from a set of gates built in honour of Assyrian King Shalmeneser III, who took the throne in 859. They show the king's soldiers assaulting a city in Syria

Slingers (top) and bow-armed charioteers (below) similar to those in the army of Shalmeneser III

THE Sun

THOUGHT: GILT COMPLEX

SILLY GOLD FOOL

Midas turns own daughter into statue

By FRANK LEE GREEDY

THIS is the moment when dopey King Midas turned his daughter into a gold statue — simply by touching her.

Midas, 58, was given the strange power after he begged the gods to satisfy his insatiable craving for gold.

But the barmy old duffer forgot to tell his beautiful daughter Zoe, 21, about his superhuman ability.

So when he tried to give her a peck on the cheek yesterday morning she ended up solid as a rock. Last night Midas was desperately trying to contact the gods in a bid to bring Zoe back to life.

An aide at his palace in Phrygia said: "He's been praying away for hours now, but no one seems to be answering. He's getting frantic."

A spokesman for the gods said: "I'm afraid mortals do have a habit of not thinking things through."

Golden Blunder — Page 23

776 BC

THE FIRST OLYMPICS

THE ancient Olympic Games, first staged in 776BC, were part of a religious festival for the god Zeus. The games were held every four years at Olympia in southern Greece.

Olympia was dedicated to the worship of Zeus and boasted a fabulous temple that was thought to mark a spot where one of his thunderbolts struck the Earth.

At first the games took place on one day and consisted solely of running races and wrestling.

But by the beginning of the 7th Century BC it had expanded to include other events like chariot and horse racing. By 472BC the games took place over five days.

The first was given over to religious rites in honour of Zeus. The day ended with competitors and judges promising to see fair play was upheld.

The second day began with chariot and horse races before moving on to the pentathlon, in which athletes competed in five sports — discus and javelin throwing, long jump, running and wrestling.

Contests for young boys dominated the third day. The fourth day started with the men's running races. These took place across three different distances, the first similar to our 200metre sprints, the second like our 400metre races and the third a long distance race of up to 4,600metres.

Jumping, wrestling, boxing and a contest called pankration — a mixture of boxing and wrestling — followed the races. The finale of the fourth day, and the final contest of the games, was the gruelling race for men in armour.

During this contest, warriors sprinted 750metres wearing a bronze helmet and leg guards and carrying a large round shield.

Modern historians have calculated that the armour must have weighed around 60lb. The final day of the games was given over to celebrations in the name of Zeus — and a banquet for the victors.

The contests took place in a rectangular area called the Stadion — a Greek term which gives us the word stadium — just a few yards from the Temple of Zeus.

The Olympic Games were only open to men and boys of Greek descent. But athletes travelled hundreds of miles from Greek colonies founded as far away as Spain, Turkey, Egypt and the Black Sea coast. The athletes competed as individuals rather than in teams from a specific city or area.

Victors did not win money or treasures — but crowns made of olive leaves. The Olympic Games thrived for more than a thousand years, reaching the height of popularity between 500BC and 300BC.

The games continued to be held up until 393AD, when the Roman emperor Theodosius I, a devout Christian, scrapped them because they celebrated a pagan god.

The modern Olympic Games were launched in the Greek capital Athens in 1896.

A statue of an athlete holding a discus, left

Two athletes set to compete with discus and javelin

THE CELTS

SCHOLARS have spent more than 100 years arguing about the date at which the first Celts arrived in Britain from continental Europe.

Some have claimed that their first migration took place as early as 2000BC.

But most now accept that the first arrivals took place somewhere between 800BC and 700BC.

When the Celts did begin to migrate they clearly came in considerable numbers because they seem to have swiftly overwhelmed the existing peoples of Britain.

Some historians believe that the Celts bypassed Britain at first, sailing instead to Ireland and setting up kingdoms there.

Whatever the date of their arrival, the Celts had a huge impact.

They were the first to introduce the concept of horse transport to these islands and the first to use spoked wheels.

But perhaps most importantly, the Celts brought their considerable iron-working skills with them.

The Celts were also extremely skilled at making clothes from wool, which were coloured with a series of vegetable dyes.

Celtic cloaks were highly-prized among fashionable Romans.

These were usually patterned with stripes or squares and were the ancestors of the Scottish plaids and tartans.

Left, runners in full armour on an Athenian vase from the sixth century BC. Right, a victorious athlete is crowned with olive leaves by the winged goddess of victory

Fighters slug it out in Pankration, a mixture of boxing and wrestling

...Timeline...

800 Start of the Iron Age in Europe. Its earliest societies are known as Hallstatt cultures; Rise of aristocracies throughout Greece; Celts begin to arrive in Britain from Europe — earliest British hillforts are built soon after their arrival.

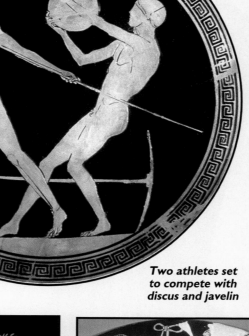

THE Sun

THOUGHT: ARMS RACE

They're OFF!

Fleeing . . . a Celtic migrant

Invasion by bogus asylum seekers

EXCLUSIVE by EMMA GRATIAN

A SUN investigation has revealed that thousands of bogus asylum-seekers are pouring into Britain every day.

Large groups of men, women and children known as Celts are arriving from across the Channel by boat.

They claim they have been forced to flee here to escape persecution.

And they say they have been forced to endure a nightmare of constant hot weather and fancy food on the continent.

Soft

But a Sun probe has discovered the Celts simply plan to impose themselves on the rest of us and take over the running of Britain.

One Celtic insider said last night: "We think Britain is a bit of a soft touch. We could easily beat up the locals and live like kings."

Luckily the Celts are easy to spot thanks to their habit of wearing garishly-patterned clothes called plaid or tartan.

WOULD YOU BE GLAD TO BE CLAD IN PLAID

See Page 19

Wacky 'Warriors Race' launches the first-ever Olympics

THE first Olympic Games got under way yesterday — with a 750-metre sprint for men wearing ARMOUR and carrying WEAPONS.

The gruelling warriors' race was the highlight of the games, held near the Temple of Zeus in Olympia, Greece.

Before contestants set off they were warned **NOT** to hurl their spears at opponents if they feared they were getting left behind.

In the end there were no casualties — but the result is still a mystery because the winner was too exhausted to tell judges his name. The rest

By DICK ATHLON

of the games were taken up with more running races — this time without the shields and swords — and wrestling matches.

Last night a spokesman for the organisers said the one-day games had been a huge hit.

Olympia now hopes to host the contest every four years — and increase the sports on offer to include boxing, javelin-throwing, jumping and chariot racing.

At the moment the games are only open to Greek athletes but Britain hopes to be invited to compete in the near future.

Synchronised Stabbing Results — Back Page

SECRETS OF A LOVE GODDESS

Read Aphrodite's saucy story in The Sun next week

ZEUS SORTS IT

EVERY Saturday top immortal Zeus sorts out your personal problems — giving advice on everything from keeping your spear shiny to waging war on a neighbouring city.

3-headed mutt makes life Hell

Dear Zeus

I LIVE on the banks of the lovely River Styx, quite close to the gates of Hell.

It's a beautiful spot and my wife and I are happy there — despite the fetid smells of sulphur that seep out of the underworld.

However, our peace and quiet has recently been shattered by the constant yelping of a three-headed dog belonging to our neighbour Hades, the owner of Hell.

Hades bought the dog, which he has named Cerberus, to guard his gates following a series of burglaries. But because the dog has three heads, one is always awake — leading to non-stop noise.

Normally this is minor yelping and whining. But when the souls of the dead are ferried across the river Cerberus goes berserk — barking fit to bust with all three mouths. My wife and I are at our wits' end. We haven't had a decent night's sleep for weeks.

■ **ZEUS SAYS:** How awful! I do sympathise with you, although strictly speaking, immortals like me do not need any sleep. I suggest you have a quiet word with Hades. If that doesn't work, why not hire a hero to hack off the dog's heads? You can probably find a suitable one in the Yellow Papyrus.

DID I WED MY MUM?

Dear Zeus

I THINK I may have married my mum by mistake.

I was abandoned as a tot and never knew my parents.

I recently married a woman who is 20 years older than me. Now I've noticed we look uncannily alike.

She also keeps saying things like: "Go and tidy your room, Oedipus."

■ **ZEUS SAYS:** I'm sure your fears are unfounded. Take care you don't develop a complex.

Should I dump my old man for sexy Troy boy

Dear Zeus

I HAVE been happily married to the wealthy King of Sparta for a couple of years — but now I fear my head has been turned by a sexy toyboy from Troy.

My husband Menelaus is kind, brave and generous but there is quite an age difference — I am 27 and he is 43.

Recently, we threw a huge banquet for local bigwigs and the King of Troy sent his hunky 25-year-old son called Paris.

Throughout the dinner he kept paying me compliments and staring at me. I thought it was a bit strange, but I put it down to the lad's outlandish foreign ways.

After dinner my husband and his guests went out into the garden to throw some javelins while I retired to the olive grove to strum a lyre. Suddenly, I was aware of someone standing behind me. As I turned I was stunned to see Paris, who had slipped away from the others and was still clutching his javelin.

Before I could speak, he took me in his arms and kissed me. I am ashamed to say that I responded — and enjoyed every second.

Now Paris wants me to leave my husband and run off to Troy with him.

I would love to go, but I fear I may start an international incident. What should I do?

■ **ZEUS SAYS:** We gods rarely feel the need to behave morally. Indeed I myself have seduced many a mortal woman under false pretences.

Once I even disguised myself as a swan to get my wicked way (but that's another story!).

If I were you, I'd go for it. After all, what is your husband going to do? Attack the city of Troy?

I WORRY THAT HEEL BE KILLED

Dear Zeus

I AM terribly worried about my son Achilles. He gets in all sorts of scraps and keeps coming home battered and bruised.

He insists it doesn't matter as he is invincible.

But I know that a simple wound in an unimportant spot like the heel could turn septic and kill him.

■ **ZEUS SAYS:** It's natural for mums to worry.

But it's also natural for healthy lads to rape, pillage and parade around with their enemies' heads on a spear.

Don't worry. He'll come to no harm.

Howls about that then . . . shepherd Faustulus brings his wife to see the wolf suckle the twin baby boys

LOST KIDS ARE RAISED BY A WOLF

Shepherd finds twin baby boys

A STUNNED shepherd yesterday found two baby boys in a wood — where they were being raised by a female WOLF.

Faustulus, 32, stumbled on the tots as he searched for a missing lamb.

He said last night: "I heard a crying noise from behind a bush. I pushed the leaves aside, thinking the lamb might be trapped — and could hardly believe my eyes.

"There on the floor were these two little mites — being suckled by this huge great wolf."

Last night the babies — believed to be twins who are about six months old — were being cared for by Faustulus and his wife Acca Larentia near the town of Alba Longa, Italy.

The wolf, who they have called

By LOU PINE

Fido, is also staying at the shepherd's hovel. Faustulus and his wife have named the tots Romulus and Remus.

No one has yet claimed the boys. But last night speculation was growing that they might be the missing nephews of Amulius, king of Alba Longa.

Incredible

Amulius, 48, staged a coup three months ago and seized the throne from his elder brother Numitor, who fled the country.

The new king then forced Numitor's daughter Silvia into exile — and seized her twin sons.

The wicked Amulius got one of his henchmen to put the babies into a basket, then cast them adrift on the River Tiber.

The tots, rumoured to have

been fathered by Mars — the god of war — had been presumed dead until now.

Faustulus said last night: "If these are the sons of Silvia it is an incredible tale.

"The she-wolf must have discovered the tots and taken pity on them, raising them as if they were her own cubs."

Faustulus and his wife now plan to raise the boys as their own if no one comes forward to claim them.

It is not known whether the wolf intends to apply for custody.

This is not the first time that a baby left on a river has been miraculously saved.

Just over 400 years ago legendary Hebrew Moses was put into the River Nile in Egypt in a wicker basket.

Luckily, he was heard crying by Pharoah's daughter who saved him and took him to her father's palace.

Homer fury over 'yob poem' jibe

TOP poet Homer has angrily denied claims that his new blockbuster glorifies mindless violence.

The poem is said to be based on the ten-year siege of Troy by the Greeks — and features many instances of graphic blood-letting.

One critic who saw an early draft of the work — provisionally titled Achilles the Terminator — said: "It's macho rubbish designed to appeal to the lowest common denominator."

But a spokesman for Homer, 45, of Chios, said last night: "There is quite a lot of fighting in it — but it's treated with great tact and taste."

Assyria set to pillage village

ASSYRIA is planning to terrorise towns and villages in neighbouring countries, political experts warned last night.

The warning comes just 50 years after Assyrian king Shalmeneser III and his chariot-riding thugs ran amok through Syria and Palestine raping and pillaging.

A spokesman for the organisation NATO — Nations Assyria Treats Offensively — said there had been a considerable build up of military personnel on Assyria's borders in recent months.

He added: "This will be especially bad news to any country that has an army smaller than Assyria's. And let's face it, that's everybody."

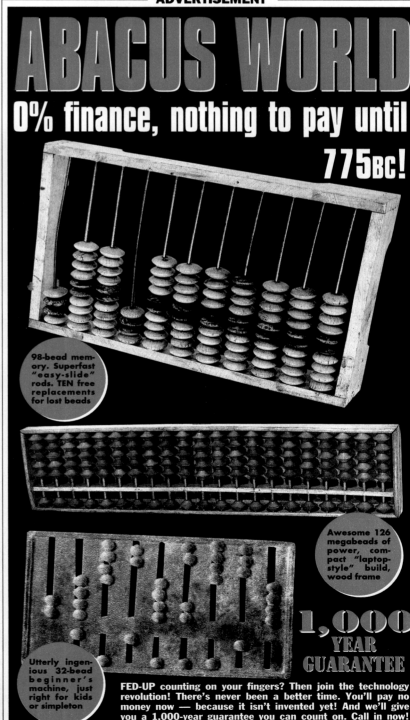
YOUR A TO Z GUIDE TO NEW ALPHABET
See Page 23

...Timeline...

774 Greeks develop phonetic alphabet, reading from left to right.

770 Start of the reign of China's Eastern Zhou dynasty.

760 Greeks found colony of Cumae in Italy.

753 Traditional date of foundation of Rome by Romulus, the city's first king — who according to legend was raised by a wolf along with his brother Remus.

743 Colonists from Corinth in Greece found city of Syracuse in Sicily.

735 Greeks begin colonisation of Sicily and Southern Italy, later known as Magna Graecia or Greater Greece.

722 Samaria, capital of Israel, falls to Assyrians.

720 Traditional date for Homer's Iliad. The Odyssey, also credited to Homer, came later.

701 Lachish (in modern-day Israel) attacked by Assyrian king Sennacherib.

700 Nomadic Cimmerian horsemen from the steppes begin raiding Asia Minor; Approximate date of Greek poet Hesiod, famous for his Theogony and Works And Days; Etruscan immigrants begin settling in area around Rome and building cities; Earliest known musical notation, in India; Gunpowder first used, in Chinese rockets; First false teeth, used by the Etruscans; First widespread use of iron in Britain. The new iron tools allow forest land to be cleared for cultivation more easily. These improved agricultural techniques and an increase in Celtic migration lead to a rapid rise in population in Britain.

687 The Lydians of western Anatolia produce crude coins and are first to open shops — the Greek historian Herodotus (born 490BC) later blasts their commercialism.

Achilles drags Hector's body behind his chariot (above) in the Iliad, written about 720. Greek vases from same period (right)

The Greek alphabet, based on a system used by the Phoenicians of the Middle East, is believed to have been introduced in 774. It was the first to use vowel symbols

687 BC

TORMENTING OF JOB

THE Old Testament character Job is synonymous with patience, thanks to his endurance of the catalogue of misfortune God inflicts on him to test his faith.

The Book of Job describes him as a rich man living in Uz. He has seven sons, three daughters, 7,000 sheep, 3,000 camels, 500 oxen, 500 donkeys and many servants. But he is also a good man who praises God at every opportunity.

God, chatting with Satan, points out what a "blameless and upright" fellow Job is. But Satan speculates that he only praises God because he has been blessed with wealth — and argues that if Job's possessions are removed he will be quick to bad-mouth the Almighty.

So God invites Satan to inflict a string of tragedies on Job to test the theory. First, thieves steal his oxen and donkeys and kill his servants. Next, a great fire from heaven kills his sheep and the servants tending them. More bandits take his camels and slaughter yet more servants. Finally wind blows down the house where his sons and daughters are having a party, killing them all.

Job's response is not to curse God. Instead he tears his clothes, shaves his head, falls on the ground and worships him, saying: "The Lord gave and the Lord has taken away."

God points out to Satan that Job has remained righteous even in the face of such adversity. So Satan urges God to allow him to inflict personal bodily harm on Job and see how he likes that.

Satan gives Job terrible sores from head to foot. But despite his wife's pleadings for him to curse God and die rather than endure further torment, Job refuses.

By the time his three horrified friends arrive to visit him he is unrecognisable and sitting in a pile of his own dung.

Job's friends tell him, in turn, that he must have done something to deserve such ill-treatment. He insists he hasn't and begs God to explain the unfairness of it all to him. Job's fourth friend even finds fault in that, saying that by questioning

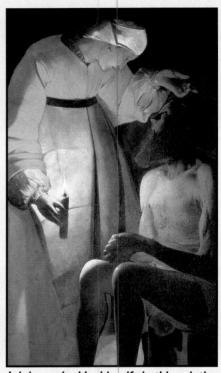

Job is mocked by his wife in this painting by Georges de la Tour from around 1650

God's judgement he is sinning. Finally God speaks. He challenges Job to explain how the universe was put together and implies he should not have the nerve to try to understand God's motives.

Job, even further humbled, admits this was a mistake and says he now hates himself.

God is happy with this, and ticks Job's friends off for not being as humble as Job. He then restores Job's wealth and doubles it, giving him back his kids and allowing him to live happily to a ripe old age.

The Book of Job, part of the Wisdom literature of the Old Testament which includes Ecclesiastes and Proverbs, is thought to have been written between 1200BC and 250BC. It is mainly in poetic form, and its unknown author is thought to have based it on an Israelite folk story from several hundred years earlier.

THE LYDIANS

THE Lydians were the greatest businessmen in the ancient world — inventing both coins and shops. They lived in western Anatolia in Turkey and were masters of Asia Minor between 650BC and 550BC.

The Lydians came up with shops and coins at roughly the same time. The ideas are obviously linked, but historians disagree on which came first. The early coins were made from electrum — a mix of gold and silver.

The Lydians were a huge influence on the Greeks, who soon began producing their own coins.

Not all Greeks admired the Lydians. The historian Herodotus criticised them for "gross commercialism."

THE Sun

Saturday, March 21, 687BC   Price: One "Coin"   **THOUGHT: SORELY TEMPTED**

PRANK THE LORD

It's tough, Job, but someone's got to do it . . . three pals try to console fallen tycoon yesterday after latest mishap. He still won't renounce his faith

God plays practical jokes on loyal Job

By TESS TAFAITH

HAPLESS former tycoon Job was still refusing to curse God last night despite the Lord inflicting yet another disastrous prank on him.

God has already swiped Job's entire fortune and wiped out all his children.

Now the celestial "joker" has afflicted him with terrible sores from head to foot. Three friends who yesterday visited Job at his home in Uz barely recognised him.

His wife has even begged him to **DIE** rather than suffer any longer.

Ironically God is thought to be making Job suffer because he **LIKES** him.

The Lord is said to be trying to prove to Satan that Job is so righteous

he will never curse God no matter how bad his troubles become.

Satan maintains that if his life and his ill-health become unbearable enough, Job **WILL** bad-mouth the deity.

So far God's theory seems to be holding up. One commentator said last night: "This Job is incredible. He's stuck it out through thick and thin.

"Job is going to become a byword for patience."

Zero Job Satisfaction — Page 9

200,574 DAYS TO GO

549 BC

PYTHAGORAS

Greek philosopher Pythagoras played a crucial role in the birth of mathematics as we know it. He is probably most famous for the Pythagorean Theorem, which says the square of the hypotenuse (the length of the longest side) of a right-angled triangle is equal to the sum of the squares of the other two sides.

Pythagoras was born in about 580BC on Samos, an Aegean island, and travelled widely for most of his life before settling, around 530BC, in Crotona, a Greek colony in southern Italy. He attracted a band of disciples inspired by his teachings on religion, politics and philosophy. What we know of Pythagoras' beliefs is entirely deduced from their writings since none of his survived. In fact, it is possible that several of the principles and discoveries attributed to him are theirs.

The group believed in immortality and that souls come back in new bodies. Pythagoras claimed to have fought in the Trojan War in a past life.

They were vegetarians, but were banned from eating beans because Pythagoras suspected they had souls.

The origins of mathematics are actually found long before Pythagoras. Early man counted by making notches on sticks or pieces of bone. The Egyptians were calculating areas and volumes about 2700BC. They counted in tens, hundreds and thousands, probably because we have ten fingers and thumbs. The Babylonians also counted in tens, but also in 60s — something we still use with hours, minutes and seconds, as well as measurements in degrees.

Much later, Pythagoras and the Greeks he inspired began to see maths as a theoretical discipline — as it is studied now. In other words, instead of working simply with sums, they developed abstract formulae to prove theories. For example, the simple formula a x b = c. From that, it follows that c/a = b, and that c/b = a.

Pythagoras and his followers studied odd and even numbers, prime numbers and square numbers. They believed numbers were the basis of everything, notably music and astronomy.

They were the first to speculate that Earth revolved around the sun, a theory only proven centuries later.

Pythagoras died in about 500BC. He was a profound influence on later mathematicians such as Euclid, Apollonius of Perga and Archimedes, and philosophers like Plato.

The Wailing Wall in Jerusalem, site of the Temple razed by Nebuchadnezzar in 586

Lawgiver Solon, who introduced wide-reaching political and economic reforms to Athens in 594

...Timeline...

681 Essarhaddon begins reign as king of Assyria.

679 Assyrians defeat Cimmerians.

672 Assyrians conquer Egypt.

668 Assurbanipal begins reign in Assyria.

663 Egypt overthrows Assyrians.

652 Gyges, king of Lydia in Asia minor, is killed by Cimmerians.

650 Tyrants begin to gain control of major cities in Greece.

640 The Lydians produce coin made of electrum, an amalgam of gold and silver.

621 Draco introduces tough legal system at Athens — we still use the word Draconian to describe repressive measures.

616 Tarquinius Priscus, Rome's first Etruscan king, comes to power.

612 Collapse of Assyrian empire and rise of Babylonians in the subsequent political vacuum.

609 More than 120,000 die trying to build a new canal from the Nile to the Red Sea.

605 Nebuchadnezzar becomes Babylonian ruler.

600 Greeks found city of Massalia (modern Marseilles) in southern France; Rough date of the Greek Pythius, first merchant banker about whom there are records; Scientist Thales of Miletos says all life came from water.

597 Nebuchadnezzar II of Babylon conquers Jerusalem. Its citizens are taken to Babylon to be slaves; Large numbers of hill forts built across Britain by Celtic tribal groups — a sign that conflict is on the increase as a rising population creates pressure for the farmland.

595 Use of coins spreads from Lydia to Greece, being first minted in Aegina.

594 Solon introduces economic and political reforms at Athens.

592 First ship anchor used by Anarcharis of Scythia, central Asia.

586 Nebuchadnezzar destroys Temple of Jerusalem.

585 Eclipse of the sun on May 28 is accurately predicted by Greek scientist Thales.

575 Coins minted in Athens.

570 Coins minted in Corinth.

561 Croesus crowned king of Lydia — his name becomes synonymous with fabulous wealth.

560 Tyrant Pisistratus seizes power in Athens.

559 Cyrus the Great becomes king of Persia (modern-day Iran).

Hillforts like this one at Maiden Castle, Dorset, were built from the 590s onwards

Scientist Thales accurately predicted an eclipse of the sun on May 28, 585. This was the one in 1999

THE Sun

Friday, June 28, 549BC   One Coin   THOUGHT: BRIGHT ANGLE

Scrolls for schools

- ● **SCROLL** up! Scroll up! The Sun today launches a brain-meltingly brilliant offer — FREE scrolls for schools.

  We know schools are hard up at the moment, and we're the first paper anywhere to do something about it. In fact, we're the first paper anywhere. Now, by collecting daily tokens in The Sun you can supply your kids' school with scrolls packed with wisdom and written on top-quality parchment.

- ● It's fun, it's a stroke of genius and it starts today, only in The Sun. Collect Token One on Page 20

MATHS MURDER
Kids' hell as boffin invents
baffling theory on triangles

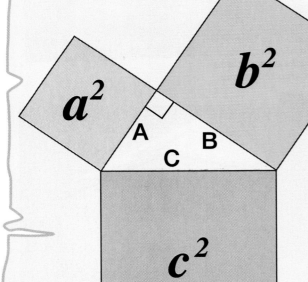

Boxing clever . . . two little 'uns put together have the same area as big 'un

By TROY HARDER, Education Correspondent

A **GREEK** philosopher has condemned generations of schoolchildren to hellish maths lessons by inventing a formula for working out things to do with triangles.

Cult leader Pythagoras, 31, has figured out that the square of the hypotenuse of a right-angled triangle is equal to the sum of the squares of the other two sides.

This has enormous implications for the world — but mainly for children who will be forced to study it.

Our graphic (left) attempts to illustrate the theory.

The hypotenuse is the triangle's longest side, the one joined to the very big box. If you add together the areas of the boxes attached to the shorter two sides, they equal the bigger one.

This is said to be tremendously important — and last night experts predicted it will open the floodgates for a host of maths problems which kids worldwide will have to solve.

Potty Pythagoras is no stranger to The Sun.

Two years ago we revealed on Page Three how he had instructed his vegetarian followers never to eat beans in case they contained **SOULS.**

He also believes he fought in the Trojan War in a past life.

The only ray of hope for children is that he refuses to write his teachings down — so there's a good chance they may be forgotten.

Madcap . . . Pythagoras

Triangle Theory In Full — Page 2

528 BC

LIFE OF BUDDHA

BUDDHA'S teachings inspired a worldwide religion that is today estimated to have between 150 and 300 million followers.

Buddhism teaches that life is full of suffering which is often caused by a craving for worldly goods.

The suffering can only be completely overcome if Buddhists abandon their worldly desires and, through contemplation and meditation, achieve a state of enlightenment known as nirvana.

The facts about the historical Buddha have often been obscured by later myth and legend.

But historians largely agree that he was born in Nepal in about 563BC into an aristocratic family of warriors.

His real name was Gautama

Siddhartha, Buddha being a later title meaning Enlightened One.

In his early years Buddha lived the life of a young aristocrat, but found it unfulfilling and was increasingly drawn to meditation and contemplation.

When he was 29 he is said to have come across an old man, a sick man and the body of a dead man during a journey.

Legend says that he suddenly realised that mankind is full of suffering. Shortly afterwards he met a wandering monk and noticed how calm the man seemed.

He decided to abandon his life of luxury and dedicate himself to seeking truth. Buddha spent years wandering around India taking instruction from Hindu teachers. But he disliked some

aspects of Hinduism and finally abandoned it.

Some time around 528BC, Buddha experienced the Great Enlightenment while sitting under a tree. He then preached his first sermon, which outlined the basic principles of what was to become Buddhism.

Buddha spent the next 40 years teaching and founding monasteries.

He died in Nepal at the age of about 80 after eating contaminated pork.

After Buddha's death there was a split among his followers over the correct way to continue his teachings.

One group believed that only monks who concentrated on seeking personal enlightenment for themselves could effectively practice Buddhism. They

called themselves Theravadan, or The Way Of The Elders.

A second group believed the teaching must be available to all people, not just monks. They called themselves Mahayana, meaning the Big Raft.

The concept of the raft came from the Buddha himself. He referred to his teaching as a raft which could help people cross to the other shore beyond birth and death.

Today Buddhism based on the Theravadan model is found in Sri Lanka, Burma, Thailand and Cambodia.

Mahayan Buddhism is the norm in China, Japan, Tibet and Korea.

In later years the Mahayan group again divided into several strands, including Zen Buddhism, which places great emphasis on meditation.

Left, a statue of Buddha at the temple of Borobudur, Java. Right, a monk walks past a statue of a reclining Buddha at Polonnaruwa, Sri Lanka. Buddhism has up to 300million followers

...Timeline...

548 Temple of Apollo at Delphi is burned down.

546 Cyrus the Great, king of Persia, begins conquest of Asia Minor.

539 Cyrus captures Babylon — he allows Jewish exiles held captive there to return home and rebuild the Temple in Jerusalem.

535 King Servius Tullius, according to tradition the sixth king of Rome, builds a wall around the city.

530 Greece has a fully-working library.

The Greek god Apollo, whose temple at Delphi was burned to the ground in 548

The tomb of Cyrus the Great in Pasargadae, Iran. Cyrus, founder of the ancient Persian empire, began conquering Asia Minor in 546

EAT YOUR WAY TO HAPPINESS
PAGES 20 & 21

THE Sun

FREE
PEACE AND ENLIGHTENMENT FOR EVERY READER
SEE CENTRE PAGES

Thursday, October 31, 528BC   One Coin   THOUGHT: FOOD

YOU BUDDHA BELIEVE IT!
Fat boy Sid starts new religion

By THEO LOGICAL

A TUBBY drifter named Sid has launched a new religion that claims everyone can be happy — as long as they give away their possessions.

Sid, 34, whose full name is Sid-dhartha Gautama, says people are made miserable because of their "worldly desires."

And he tells his followers they'll be a lot more cheerful if they dump all their trinkets and spend more time being nice to people and animals.

Sid, who weighs in at about 15st, has spent the last few years wandering around India.

He is already building up quite a following of admirers. They call him

Buddha — which means the Enlightened One — and refer to his religion as Buddhism.

Bizarrely, although Buddhism claims to be a religion it features NO human sacrifice, NO ritual slaughter of animals and NO Sun worship.

Instead, believers simply have to sit very still and spend time thinking — a practice called meditation.

Last night a spokesman for BAD, the British Association of Druids, predicted the new religion would be a flop.

He said: "All this peace and happiness is all very well, but what people really want from a religion is blood, blood and more blood."

Predict Your Own Future Using A Sheep's Intestines — Page 15

508 BC

DEMOCRACY IN ATHENS

ANCIENT Greece was made up of a series of individual city states, each with its own laws, customs and political systems.

While these cities would often club together to form alliances in times of conflict, they were essentially independent.

Most of the city states had initially been ruled by kings.

But by about 750BC the wealthier sections of society had seized power. The Greeks called this form of government oligarchy, or the rule of the few. In some cities, rivalries among the ruling nobles led to bloodshed. Sometimes one aristocrat would appeal directly to the mass of the poorer citizens for support, promising to end the unrest if they helped him seize sole power.

These aristocrats were called tyrants (in ancient Greece the word was not used as a term of loathing, but simply to describe a system of government.)

In 560BC a tyrant called Pisistratus seized power amid an economic crisis in Athens.

He passed laws which reduced the power of the nobility at the same time as increasing the role of the ordinary citizen in the running of the city.

Pisistratus ruled for 30 years. When he died his sons Hippias and Hipparchus took power. In the years that followed Athens plunged into chaos. Hipparchus was assassinated and Hippias fled in terror to Athens' traditional enemy, the city of Sparta.

Sparta twice invaded Athens and set up short-lived puppet rulers.

But in 508BC the Athenian aristocrat Cleisthenes became the effective ruler and began introducing laws to make the city a democracy. Under his system the main arm of the government was the Council of 500.

Every male citizen was eligible to sit on the council and its members were chosen by lot.

The Council was regulated by the Assembly, made up of all the other male citizens. It was allowed to veto any of the Council's proposals.

The Assembly alone had the right to declare war.

In 487BC a new law was passed aimed at stopping ambitious politicians from seizing power. This allowed the Assembly to vote to expel a citizen from the state for a period of ten years. The practice was known as ostracism.

Democracy thrived in Athens in the years following Cleisthenes' reforms.

The revolutionary ideas gave ordinary citizens the right to vote on government policies, hold political office, elect military leaders and serve on a jury.

However, the reforms did not give power to all those living in Athens. Women were excluded as were the many thousands of slaves working in the city and its surrounding areas.

And the large numbers of so-called metics, foreigners who lived and traded in Athens, had no rights.

Democracy in Athens was effectively ended in 338BC when Philip of Macedon defeated its army at the battle of Chaeronea — making himself master of Greece.

Relics of democracy. Pieces of pottery (left) on which Athenians wrote the names of those they wished exiled, small discs (right) bearing the names of potential jurors and (centre) a device into which the discs were slotted before being picked at random

Carving at the Persian capital Persepolis showing the Royal court of Darius, who became king in 521

Subjects from across the enormous Persian empire are shown on this relief bringing tributes to Darius

...Timeline...

525 The Persians conquer Egypt.

521 Darius I made king of Persia.

520 Building of new Temple in Jerusalem begins.

514 Attempt to assassinate Athenian tyrant Hippias is foiled — his brother Hipparchus is later killed.

510 Tyranny overthrown at Athens after Hippias is ousted by the army of Sparta, southern Greece.

508 Cleisthenes begins a series of political reforms that introduce democracy to Athens.

A bronze statuette of a young Greek man reclining at a drinking party with a wine cup in his hand. The figure dates from the late 6th Century BC — a time when the tyrants of Athens were being replaced with a democratic system

THE Sun

Thursday, January 7, 508BC   One Coin   THOUGHT: IT'S A-POLLING

MOB RULE

Point of disorder . . . Athenians quarrel yesterday over who will count the votes. The man at the front is sulking because he claims it is his turn

Crazy Greeks give power to the people

By MARK YERCROSS
Political Editor

CRAZED Greeks have come up with a new political system — that lets the PEOPLE rule.

The insane idea, known as democracy, has been introduced in the city of Athens.

From now on **EVERY** citizen will have a say in running the place — even those who are extremely poor. They will be able to attend all political meetings and raise their hands if they agree with proposals, a system known as "voting."

Up until now Athens has been like most other cities in the world — ruled by cruel tyrants who insist on every whim being obeyed and demand to be worshipped like gods. This time-honoured method has proved immensely popular as it ensures political stability and stops the rabble from getting uppity.

Aristocrats in Athens said last night that they will continue to oppose the reforms.

A spokesman said: "It's horrific, but it could have worse. At least they didn't give the vote to women."

You The Jury: Should People Have The Right To Vote? — Page Eight

174,902 DAYS TO GO

480BC

THE 300 SPARTANS

A 19th Century picture of Sparta's King Leonidas, who died with 300 of his men while fighting the Persians at Thermopylae in 480

Chinese scholars were writing on bamboo from about 500

...Timeline...

507 Last Etruscan king, Tarquinius Superbus, is expelled from Rome. City becomes a republic.

500 Greeks have a telegraph based on hilltop fires, mirrors and shouting; A kind of "Pony Express" is operating in Persia; Chinese scholars writing on bamboo — their pens are reeds dipped in pigment; Britain's population thought to have hit 1.5million around this time.

499 Cities set up by Greek colonists in Ionia (western Turkey) rebel against their Persian overlords.

496 Birth of Athenian playwright Sophocles, author of Oedipus Rex; Romans defeat Latins at battle of Lake Regillus.

494 Common people of Rome (the plebeians) threaten to leave the city if they are not granted more political power by the aristocratic families (the patricians). The patricians agree to create a number of new officials, called tribunes, to protect the people's interests; Ionian revolt crushed by Persian army.

493 Themistocles is archon (chief minister) at Athens.

490 Persians invade mainland Greece but are beaten by Athenian army at Battle of Marathon.

488 Gelon, ruler of Sicilian city of Gela, wins chariot race at Olympic games.

485 Xerxes becomes king of Persia; Birth of Athenian dramatist Euripides.

480 Xerxes invades Greece. Spartan King Leonidas and 300 of his men try to block the Persians' path through a mountain pass at Thermopylae but are overwhelmed and killed; Athenians abandon their city to the Persians, who burn the temples on the Acropolis; Persian fleet defeated by Athenians and their allies off the island of Salamis; Birth of Greek historian Herodotus.

Persian soldier from the army of King Xerxes, who invaded Greece in 490 and 480

A modern reconstruction of an ancient Athenian trireme — one of the warships used by Themistocles to defeat the Persian fleet at the battle of Salamis in 480

THE heroic last stand by 300 Spartans at the Battle of Thermopylae is the most famous incident from the Persians' failed attempt to conquer Greece in 480BC.

The Persian king Xerxes had invaded northern Greece with a vast army. The Greek city states knew they were hopelessly outnumbered and dared not risk open battle.

So they decided to meet the Persian army at Thermopylae — a mountain pass that it would have to use if it was to march into central Greece.

The pass itself was barely 50ft across at its narrowest point — the perfect point for a small army to fight a much larger one on equal terms.

The Greeks put their forces under the command of Leonidas, king of the warlike Spartans of southern Greece.

The Greeks totalled no more than 10,000, including servants.

The Persian army was said by the ancient Greek historian Herodotus to number an improbable 1.75million. The true figure is unknown, but Xerxes' army was many times larger than that of the Greeks.

The Persians attacked the pass of Thermopylae for two days, but the Spartans and their allies held firm. However, a traitor showed Xerxes a secret mountain path which would allow him to attack the Spartans from behind. Leonidas learned of the betrayal but refused to retreat.

Instead, he sent most of his troops to safety before they were encircled, while he remained with 300 Spartans.

The king and his followers were attacked from front and rear, and overwhelmed. None survived.

But the delaying tactics had given Greece a vital breathing space. The Athenians were able to evacuate every man, woman and child from the city before the Persians arrived.

Within weeks the tables were turned on Xerxes as a mainly Athenian fleet decisively defeated the Persian navy at the battle of Salamis.

In the following year Xerxes abandoned the invasion attempt when his army was routed by the Spartan commander Pausanias.

The Greeks never forgot the heroism of the 300 Spartans. At the pass of Thermopylae they set up a memorial with a carved inscription that read:

"Tell them in Sparta thou who pass by,

That here, obedient to their laws, we lie."

THE Sun

Saturday, March 21, 480BC   One Coin   THOUGHT: LEO THE LION

HEROES TO THE LAST MAN

300 Spartans killed

By DI FIGHTING

A BRAVE band of Spartan soldiers who tried to stop a huge Persian horde from invading Greece were last night all feared to have been butchered.

The 300 heroes, led by the Spartan king Leonidas, tried to block the path of a Persian army believed to number almost **TWO MILLION.**

They occupied a mountain pass the Persians needed to get through in Thermopylae, central Greece, and refused to budge.

Despite the overwhelming odds the Spartans kept their enemies at bay for more than two days. But a traitor showed the Persian king Xerxes a secret path through the mountains — and his men surrounded the Spartans in the dark.

LAUGHED

Last night locals reported that the plucky spearmen had **REFUSED** to surrender — preferring instead to die with honour.

One said: "They didn't stand a chance, but they just laughed in the Persians' faces when they were told to throw down their spears and shields."

No Xpense Spared: Xerxes' Luxury Lifestyle — Pages Eight and Nine

Defiant . . . a Spartan soldier prepares to face the Persian army

...Timeline...

The philosopher Socrates prepares to commit suicide in 399 by swallowing poison. The picture was painted by the 19th Century French artist Jacques Louis David

479 Sparta and her allies defeat Persians at battle of Plataea.

477 Athens and her allies form Confederacy of Delos — a body designed to ensure mutual support. Dominance of Athens soon transforms it into an empire.

472 First performance of The Persians, a tragedy by great Athenian dramatist Aeschylus.

470 Work begins on temple of Zeus at Olympia; Birth of philosopher Socrates.

465 Earthquake at Sparta — it is followed by a revolt of the helots, the oppressed peasants.

460 Athenians send fleet and troops to Egypt in support of a rebellion against Persian rulers; Birth of Greek historian Thucydides and Greek doctor Hippocrates.

458 Athens begins building Long Walls around city and its harbour Piraeus.

457 Birth of comic writer Aristophanes.

454 Athens' Egyptian expedition ends in disaster; Athenian statesman Pericles begins rise to power; Athens starts demanding tribute payments from cities within her empire.

451 Collection of Roman laws, known as the Twelve Tables, is published. Pericles restricts Athenian citizenship to those who have a mother and father who are Athenians.

447 Work begins on the Parthenon, Athens.

440 Democritus thinks up the concept of atom to describe the smallest particles of matter which make up universe; Historian Herodotus visits Egypt.

431 Start of Peloponnesian War between Athens and Sparta for control of Greece.

430 Outbreak of plague at Athens — it may have killed 30,000, a sixth of population.

429 Death of Pericles; Birth of philosopher Plato.

428 Birth of Greek writer and soldier Xenophon.

The Parthenon, Athens. The temple, for the goddess Athena, was begun in 447

Democritus suggested the universe was made up of tiny atoms as early as 440

424 Historian Thucydides is banished from Athens because of a military blunder.

415 Athens send expedition to Sicily to attack Sparta's allies. It ends in disaster.

405 Spartan general Lysander destroys Athenian navy at battle of Aegospotomai.

404 Athens surrenders to Sparta, ending the Peloponnesian War.

401 Some 10,000 Greek mercenaries, led by Xenophon, march into Asia Minor to support a doomed rebellion by the Persian king's brother Cyrus.

400 Chinese are writing on silk and using crossbow.

399 Socrates sentenced to death for "corrupting the young" with his philosophy. He commits suicide by taking poison.

390 The Gauls, a Celtic people, swarm south into Italy and sack Rome.

390 BC

PLATO & PHILOSOPHY

IN the years between 600BC and 200BC Greek civilisation and culture reached its height. More than 2,000 years later the ideas the Greeks developed are still at the centre of our way of life.

For example, each episode of EastEnders has its roots in the dramas created by ancient Greek writers.

The very idea of sport — of individuals or teams competing against each other for glory — has come down to us from the Greeks.

And our politics, music, buildings, medicine and science are based on ideals hammered out by the Greeks centuries before the birth of Christ.

The Greeks were perhaps the most inquisitive race that has ever lived. They wanted to know how the world worked; what man's role in it should be; did God exist, why did evil exist — and many other seemingly unanswerable questions.

Some of their greatest thinkers spent their lives trying to solve these problems. The Greek word for these men was philosopher, or "lover of wisdom."

Chief among them was Plato. He was born in 429BC and spent most of his life living and teaching in Athens.

As a young man he was deeply influenced by the philosopher Socrates. Socrates said that young people must think for themselves and challenge traditional beliefs. This made him unpopular in conservative Athens and in 399BC he committed suicide by drinking poison after being found guilty of corrupting the nation's youth.

Plato left Athens in disgust and spent the next decade travelling around the Mediterranean. In 387BC he returned home and set up the Academy — the first ever European university. Here he taught mathematics, science and morality.

Among his students was a brilliant young man called Aristotle, himself destined to become one of the greatest philosophers.

When Plato died in 347BC he left behind a body of written work that detailed his thoughts on a range of subjects from politics and education to art and the nature of friendship.

Many of his views on religion had a huge influence on the development of Christian thinking.

Most of Plato's works are complex. Perhaps the most confusing is his Theory of Forms.

In simple terms, Plato believed everyday objects are copies of a perfect version of that object which exists in an alternative world.

For example, all the bananas of our world are imperfect imitations of the true banana that was created by God and exists in the "perfect" world.

OLYMPIC CHEATING

THE ancient Olympics were as blighted with tales of cheating and match-fixing as modern sporting events have become.

In theory, the games at Olympia were all about amateurism, with the victors taking home nothing more than a crown of olive leaves.

But in reality there was real money at stake because Olympic champions brought glory to their home town.

It was common for victors to have all their food provided for the rest of their life, to be given cash, to be exempted from taxes or to be given top jobs. One grateful city built a wrestling champion his own private gymnasium. Because of this, many of the athletes competing in the games were full-time sportsmen who employed their own trainers — and some were willing to cheat their way to the coveted Olympic crown.

The earliest recorded cheat was Eupolus of Thessaly, who bribed boxers in the 98th Olympics.

Callippus of Athens paid off his competitors in the pentathlon during the 112th festival. Two Greek boxers, Didas and Sarapammon, were fined for fixing the outcome of their match at the 226th Olympics.

ROME AND GAULS

AROUND 400BC the Celtic tribesmen known as the Gauls began migrating south from their homes near the River Danube in search of new land.

Ten years later they invaded Roman territory — defeating a Roman army in battle before storming into the city.

Only a strongly-fortified settlement on the Capitoline Hill in the centre of Rome was able to hold out. The Gauls laid siege to the hill — and one night tried to sneak in while the Roman defenders were asleep.

But, according to legend, some geese who were kept nearby began honking when they spotted the strangers and their noise woke the guards, who drove the Gauls back.

The Gauls stayed in Rome for seven months — leaving only after they were paid a huge ransom in gold.

THE Sun

Friday, May 22, 390BC   One Coin   THOUGHT: EH?

GEESE SAVE ROME

By RAY SALARM

THE city of Rome has been saved from barbarian raiders — by a flock of geese.

A gang of the ruffians crept up to the city at night and began to climb over a defensive wall.

But some geese who were kept in a nearby temple took a gander at the hairy invaders — and began honking as loudly as they could.

The Romans were woken by the racket, grabbed their swords and chased the barbarians away.

Geesekill's View — Page Eight

Cheat . . . Eupolus in action

Olympic boxer in match-fix scandal

EXCLUSIVE

By PAULA FASTONE

OLYMPIC chiefs were last night rocked by claims that boxing champion Eupolus **CHEATED** his way to his title.

Eupolus is said to have paid his opponents in the 98th Games a series of bribes to let him win.

The sensational claims have been made by the Athens-based gambler Oddsonophon, who reckons he made a fortune when rank outsider Eupolus took the title.

Oddsonophon said last night: "I gave Eupolus 500 drachmas to bribe his opponents.

"Without the backhanders he could not have beaten an egg."

Cauliflower

Eupolus, from Thessaly, was crowned champion after knocking out Halicarnassus hardman Phormio in the final.

Phormio, who had won the boxing crown at the previous Olympics, had been hot favourite.

Boxing fans have always suspected there was something fishy about the fight.

Sun boxing correspondent Chuck Intowel said: "Eupolus was hopeless. During his career he spent so much time on the canvas he had a cauliflower backside."

Olympic chiefs are probing the claims.

Eupolus is now retired from boxing, but could still be stripped of his title.

More seriously, he could be struck by one of Zeus's thunderbolts.

Eu 'Orrible Little Man — Page 7

It's all Greek to us!

GENIUS'S THEORY IS GOBBLEDYGOOK

HIS BAFFLING BED BRAINWAVE

God, whether from choice or from necessity, made one bed in nature and one only. Two or more such ideal beds neither ever have been nor ever will be made by God. Why is that? Because even if He had made but two, a third would still appear behind them which both of them would have for their idea. God desired to be the real maker of a real bed, not a particular maker of a particular bed, and therefore He created a bed which is essentially and by nature one only. See what I mean?

My mind's a blanket . . . Plato explains why beds are so important to God

By PHIL O'SOPHIE

BARMY boffin Plato has come up with a theory that explains the secrets of the universe — but **NO ONE** can understand it.

Top thinker Plato, 49, from Athens, Greece, claims his Theory of Forms is the greatest scientific breakthrough since the discovery that the world is flat.

But an advanced copy leaked to The Sun is so baffling that we cannot make head nor tail of it. In one bit he says that nothing in our world really exists at all.

And in another section he rants on for ages about God spending all his time making beds – but some of them are not real beds at all. Or something like that.

A spokesman for Plato said last night: "I know it's all a bit confusing, but he really is very clever."

Plato is now thought to be writing a blockbuster about triangles.

SIX GREEK GEEKS AND SIX OF THE BUST - Page 8

SIX GREEK GEEKS

WE all know that the Greeks are supposed to be the cleverest blokes around — finding out how the world works, doing some tricky things with numbers and knocking up more than a few impressive buildings.

But it has to be said that some of their so-called brainboxes seem to be a few degrees short of a right-angled triangle, if you know what we mean. So today The Sun gives you its guide to the best and the worst of Greek civilisation. From the genius of storyteller Homer to the lunacy of potty philosopher Pythagoras.

First we start with our Six Greek Geeks — a handful of losers who must surely have been struck on the head by one of Zeus's thunderbolts when they were babies.

PERICLES

POLITICIAN: One of the madmen behind the ridiculous political system "democracy".

Insisted that the views of the masses must always be right. Got his come-uppance when mob turned on him during war with Sparta and accused him of embezzling state money. His girlfriend Aspasia was prosecuted for having loose morals.

DEMOCRITUS

PHILOSOPHER: Known as the laughing philosopher because of his constant inane grin.

Reckons everything is made up of millions of tiny specks of dust called atoms which are constantly whizzing around.

Apparently, these atoms are so small they cannot be seen by the naked eye — similar in many ways to his brain.

PYTHAGORAS

GENERAL NUTCASE: Difficult to know just where to start with this one.

Spent most of his life banging on about numbers and triangles.

Ranked as a genius mainly because no one ever understood a word he said.

Also thought it was wrong to eat beans — because they had feelings too.

HERODOTUS

LIAR: Wrote a book of Greek history that would only be taken seriously by the terminally insane — and the Greeks.

Among his preposterous claims was that in India giant ants dig gold out of the earth.

Also reckons Phoenician explorers actually managed to sail all the way round Africa, which is clearly impossible.

ARISTOPHANES

BORE: Man responsible for vast number of tedious plays which are supposed to make us laugh.

One of these "masterpieces" tells the side-splitting story of a group of old men who are serving on a jury.

Another tells of how a group of birds build a city in the sky. A real rib-tickler, as you can imagine.

DEMOSTHENES

ORATOR: Believe it or not, th Greeks actually love peopl who won't shut up.

And this bloke is the king o all windbags. Nicknamed Golden Gob by his fellow Athe nians, Demosthenes is famou for his ability to speak on an subject for hours on end. Sor of bloke you'd sit next to you worst enemy at a dinner party

SIX OF THE BUST

WHEN you think about the Greeks — what picture do you conjure up? Probably a group of wild-eyed individuals with straggly beards ranting on about whether the moon revolves around Uranus.

And that's just the women.

But seriously, folks, they're not all like that. Some of them are not too different from us Brits — fine, upstanding, handsome men who enjoy a bit of banter after a hard day slaughtering rival tribesmen and enslaving their womenfolk.

So here The Sun presents Six of the Bust — our guide to half-a-dozen fellas who have made Greek civilisation the envy of Europe — ranging from a hero who clubbed a lion to death to two writers whose adventure stories always top the bestsellers' list.

ARISTOTLE

GENIUS: If you want to know anything about anything, just ask Aristotle.

He's an expert on astrology, animals, astronomy, mathematics, religion and psychology.

He's also written about plants, poetry, drama and politics.

Amazingly, his teacher was potty Plato. Clearly, he never paid attention to the old boy.

HIPPOCRATES

MEDIC: Top doctor who discovered that all illness is caused by badly-digested food.

Also brought in a code for medics that ensures that they must try to do their best when treating us.

Until he came up with this too many doctors cut bits off their patients just to see what happened.

HERCULES

HERO: Toughest bloke in the world.

First hit the headlines when as an 18-year-old he beat a lion to death with a club, then skinned it.

Later, for a laugh, he killed a nine-headed swamp monster called the hydra and wrestled with Cerberus — the three-headed dog that guards Hell. Not a man to mess with!

HOMER

POET: Blind writer who penned the violent Trojan War story, the Iliad.

The thriller ends up with a body count running into thousands as both Greek and Trojan warriors get bashed, mashed and slashed.

It sold millions, despite claims that Homer was encouraging kids to be yobs.

SOPHOCLES

WRITER: Storyteller best known for his award-winning soap, Oedipus Rex.

It tells how a kid abandoned as a baby later kills his dad by accident — before unwittingly marrying his mother. Needless to say, it ends in tragedy.

Critics accused Sophocles of cheap sensationalism. Audiences loved it.

ARES

GOD: The hardman of Mount Olympus, he loves a scrap.

Ares spends most of his time trying to persuade humans to abandon diplomacy and start fighting.

When not brawling or sharpening his sword he can often been found snogging Aphrodite, even though she's married to the fire god Hephaestus.

You're giving rabble a vote? You've gotta be DEMOCRAZY

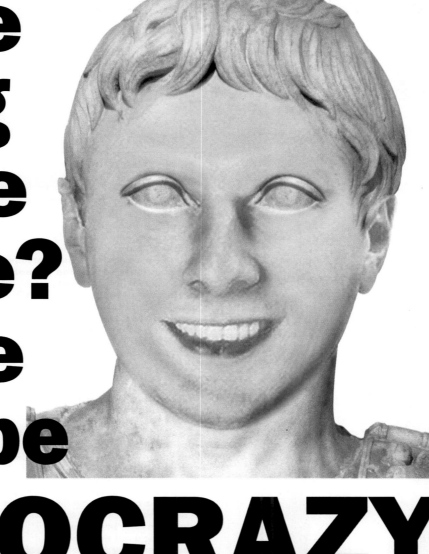

GREEKS like Plato have come up with some Mickey Mouse ideas in their time — but nothing as barking as this democracy lark.

Everyone has a say? I don't remember voting for that.

And, mark my flippin' words, it'll turn out to be just another Athenian stunt to publicise some new tragedy.

It was the same old story in Rome in 616 back in the days of Tarquinius Priscus. New ruler comes to power. And just decades later — as if by magic — a ruddy great temple suddenly appears.

All in the name of selling a few dozen more Etruscan vases.

Columns

And, believe me, they might be fashionable now, but come 300BC these so-called 'urns' will be seen for exactly what they are — a crockery of old ****.

Anyway, I've been studying this 'democracy' caper and it all seems to be down to Themistocles and Pericles. Testicles, if you ask me.

Apparently, Pericles widened democracy and restored the temples destroyed by the Persians during the second Persian war.

According to the tablets I've been reading he also "built the Parthenon on the Acropolis" — which must be news to the thousands of slaves who bust their nuts erecting those sturdy columns (ooh missus!)

And while I'm on the subject, is it just me or does Pericles look a lot like the great god Zeus?

Never see them together, do you?

Whatever. The gist of democracy is that all male Athenian citizens have been given the right to vote, serve on a jury, hold political office and roger the hell out of any good-looking man in robes.

Actually, I made that last bit up.

But a few Athenian insiders have hinted at what goes on after dark in the city — and, as we've seen from the Parthenon, those lads certainly like a big column.

So I'm stuffed if I'm going to let an Athenian enter my debating chamber.

Have to say though, it's a little bit insulting that slaves and women haven't been given the same rights . . . the slaves must be gutted.

Arf.

Actually that's incredibly sexist and bigoted.

Women should definitely be given the vote . . . just as soon as they learn to reverse-park a chariot.

Only kidding, girls . . . I wouldn't let any of you near my chariot.

However, the upshot of all this right- on cobblers is that an assembly of "elected citizens" has the none-too- thrilling task of determining government policies and electing Athenian generals.

But we don't hear the Chinese bang on about democracy, do we?

No. That's because they're too busy inventing the crossbow.

The Chinese would no more encourage democracy than they would emigrate en masse to the other half of the world to do other people's laundry.

Toilets

And, frankly, if the damn thing was worth inventing in the first place it would have been invented by one of the industrious Celtic tribes which has been colonising Britain for the last few hundred years.

Perhaps from the most northern area of that country.

Their Celtic customs and artefacts are already spreading throughout Britain and I expect great things of these inventive folk in years to come.

In the meantime a few hundred airy-fairy playwrights are chuntering away about these new-fangled flush toilets in Athens.

Cheers, fellas. But just so you know, you've not suddenly become the cradle of western civilisation — you're just talking c***.

'I wouldn't let woman near my chariot'

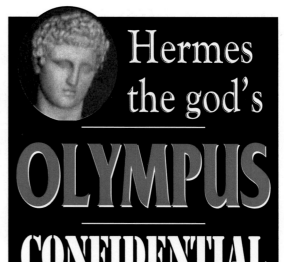

117,639 DAYS TO GO

Huntsmen pictured killing a lion in a mosaic from Pella — capital of Philip II of Macedonia, who became king in 359

323BC

ALEXANDER THE GREAT

ALEXANDER the Great is the outstanding military genius of antiquity — a seemingly-invincible general who conquered half the known world in his short life.

To the ancients he was the ultimate hero . . . unflinchingly brave, outrageously daring, generous to his enemies and devoted to his friends.

But there was a darker side to Alexander and his life story is peppered with tales of drunken brutality and bloody purges.

Alexander was born in 356BC, son of Philip II, king of the northern Greek state of Macedonia. His mother Olympias, a princess from the neighbouring country of Epirus, was rumoured to be a witch.

As a child, Alexander was taught by the great philosopher Aristotle.

Alexander became king when Philip was assassinated by a disgruntled guardsman in 336BC.

Philip had made himself master of Greece by a mixture of military might and diplomatic skill. But on news of his death revolts broke out.

Alexander used the superb Macedonian army to crush the rebels without mercy. Now he was free to attempt his father's greatest ambition — the invasion of the Persian empire, which stretched from Turkey to Egypt and India. In the spring of 334BC Alexander crossed into Turkey with about 35,000 troops. At the river Granicus he utterly defeated a 40,000-strong Persian army.

Alexander continued his advance southward until he at last met the main Persian army, led by King Darius, at Issus, north-east Syria.

The result was another crushing victory for Alexander. Darius fled, leaving behind his mother, wife and children, who were captured.

Alexander carried on moving south, storming the important Mediterranean seaports as he went. He then moved into Egypt, which was taken without a struggle.

During his stay in Egypt Alexander visited the temple of Amon, the god whom the Greeks associated with Zeus.

During this pilgrimage Alexander seemed to become convinced that Zeus was his true father, not Philip.

Alexander now left Egypt and headed north in search of Darius and his army.

He caught up with them just outside Babylon in modern-day Iraq and on October 1, 331BC, Alexander won the decisive battle of Gaugemela.

Darius again fled the battlefield, but was murdered by two of his own generals.

In the middle of winter Alexander and his army entered the Persian capital of Persepolis. During a drunken rampage he and his men set the beautiful city ablaze.

Over the next three years Alexander campaigned non-stop in the mountainous regions of modern-day Afghanistan and Turkestan.

His behaviour became increasingly despotic. During a drunken rage he killed an officer named Clitus, who had previously saved his life.

Two other leading Macedonian officers were executed for treason, as was the court historian Callisthenes.

In 327BC Alexander led his army into India, defeating King Porus at the battle of the Hydaspes. From there Alexander planned to march on to conquer China. But his men refused to go on. Reluctantly, Alexander agreed to return to Babylon.

In June 323BC, while still in Babylon, Alexander developed a fever. He was expected to recover, but a series of wounds received in battles had taken a terrible toll on his body, and he died a few days later, aged 32.

...Timeline...

386 Plato founds famous philosophical school, the Academy, in Athens.

384 Birth of philosopher Aristotle, founder of Lyceum school in Athens.

373 Temple of Delphi destroyed by earthquake.

371 Thebans defeat Spartans at battle of Leuctra.

359 Philip II becomes king of Macedonia.

356 Philip seizes cities in northern Greece and defeats neighbouring Thracians and Illyrians; Philip's son Alexander born.

353 Philip's army pushes south into Greece.

351 Demosthenes makes first of a series of speeches to the Athenians, urging them to vigorously oppose Philip.

347 Death of Plato; Athenians send embassy to Philip.

343 Philosopher Aristotle goes to Macedonia to be a tutor to Alexander.

341 The pro-peace party in Athens is defeated by the anti-Philip party of Demosthenes.

340 Philip prepares for war with Athens; Aristotle says Earth is round and space infinite.

338 Macedonian army heads south towards Athens; Athenian-Theban army defeated by Philip at Battle of Chaeronea — leaving him master of Greece.

336 Philip sends an advance force into Asia Minor to secure a bridgehead for a possible future invasion; Philip divorces Alexander's mother Olympias and marries Macedonian noblewoman — Months later Philip is assassinated; Alexander becomes king.

335 Alexander puts down revolts in Illyria, Thrace and Thebes — the city of Thebes is razed to the ground in punishment.

334 Alexander begins invasion of Persian empire — defeating army at Battle of Granicus (modern-day Turkey).

A monument commemorating the battle of Chaeronea, in central Greece, in 338

333 Macedonian army moves southwards through Asia Minor; Persians defeated for second time at Battle of Issus.

332 Alexander conquers Egypt and visits oracle Zeus at Siwa.

331 Foundation of Alexand Alexander defeats Persian army at Battle of Gaugeme

330 Alexander burns royal palaces at Persepolis; Darius is murdered by his own men.

329 Macedonians push into modern-day Afghan

327 Alexander kills Macedonian officer named Clitus during a drunken row; Alexander marries Sogdian princess Roxanne; Macedonian army enters India.

326 Alexander defeats Indian king Porus a battle of Hydaspes; Alexander plans to push on, but army refuses to march any further.

325 Macedonian army marches back towards Babylon through the desert.

323 Alexander dies of fever in Babylon.

Silver coins showing Alexander with ram's horn, symbol of Zeus

THE Sun

ALEXANDER THE GREAT
356 BC – 323 BC

Monday, June 12, 323BC   **One Coin**   **THOUGHT: DEFEATED AT LAST**

ALEX DEAD AT 32

So brave . . . Alexander rides into battle

From PETER DOUT in Babylon

ALEXANDER the Great — the warrior king dubbed the Conqueror of the World — has died in Babylon at the age of just 32.

Alex slipped into a coma after developing a fever following a party.

He was expected to recover at first, but when he was still delirious after a couple of days it was clear he was seriously ill.

Last night one of the Macedonian king's closest advisers said: "We are all stunned. Alexander was like a god. It's hard to believe that he's not here any more."

Doctors say Alexander was too weak to beat the fever because of the enormous punishment his body took over the years.

INVASION

He was notorious for being in the thick of the fighting and suffered scores of serious wounds. A few years ago he was close to death when his lung was punctured by a spear thrust during an assault on a city.

Alexander left his Macedonian home 11 years ago as he led his army on an invasion of the Persian empire — and never returned.

During that time he conquered a vast area that took in Greece, Egypt, Persia, Asia Minor and parts of India.

Alexander Couldn't Conquer His Drink Problem —
Pages Four and Five

Conqueror of world too weak to beat fever

ALEXANDER THE GREAT 356BC - 323BC

He was brave, he was wild, he conquered the world...but he couldn't conquer his drink problem

By DUNCAN DISORDERLEE

THE world is in mourning today for Alexander the Great — the handsome hero who became a legend by conquering a vast empire.

To the outside world he was as brave as a lion, merciful to his enemies and utterly unbeatable in battle.

But to his closest aides he was a brutal monster whose drunken rampages ended in the murder of his friends.

One Macedonian general, who asked not to be identified, said last night: "The truth is, Alex was uncontrollable if he had too much wine — and he had too much most nights.

"One minute he'd be the caring, considerate king we all loved. The next he'd become a raging lunatic who would strike out in blind temper at anyone who disagreed with him."

The flare-ups usually occurred when the Macedonian army ended a day of marching and made camp for the night.

Alex and his officers would get together to relax — and drink vast quantities of strong Greek wine.

Most Greeks mix this potent brew with water. But Alex and his tough soldiers liked to drink it neat.

After hours of boozing and boasting, violent rows often developed. And Alex was always in the thick of the trouble.

Berserk

During one drunken night, when the army was quartered in the city of Samarkand in Asia, Alex had a bust-up with a 36-year-old cavalry officer named Clitus — and ended up with blood on his hands. The general said:

❝No one knows how the row began, but both Clitus and Alex were pretty drunk. Suddenly I heard Clitus yell, 'Your dad was a better leader than you'.

Alex went berserk and lunged at Clitus. We grabbed both of them and held tight as they shouted abuse.

I remember Alex managed to get a hand free and grab an apple off a table.

He hurled it at Clitus and hit him on the head. Then he broke free and tried to grab his sword, but it was whisked away from him. He managed to punch Clitus in the face before we separated them. It was bedlam.

Some other officers managed to hustle Clitus out of the building while we tried to calm Alex down. But he was demented, his eyes were rolling and he was panting like a trapped beast.

Suddenly a door at the other end of the room burst open and Clitus staggered in, shouting, 'Here I am, Alexander, here I am!'

Alex grabbed a lance from one of the guards standing nearby and with a terrible yell ran straight at Clitus, spearing him through the chest. He died instantly.

The room went silent. We were all stunned.

Drunk in charge ... Alexander's all-night boozing sessions made him paranoid

Alex fell to his knees and began sobbing uncontrollably.❞

It is not surprising Alexander wept. The man he had killed was no ordinary officer.

When they were kids Clitus had been like an older brother to Alex, who was seven years his junior. Clitus's older sister had even nursed Alex when he was a baby.

And at the Battle of the River Granicus five years earlier Clitus had saved Alex's life, spearing a Persian cavalryman who was about to cut the king down. When Alex was sober the full horror of his crime became clear to him. For three days he lay on his bed sobbing, refusing all food and drink.

Passers-by heard him repeatedly wail: "I'm the murderer of my friends, the murderer of my friends."

The Macedonians tried to hush up the story. They claimed Clitus was angry because he had been passed over for promotion and had attacked Alex, who struck out in self-defence. But those in the king's inner circle knew it was not the first time too much booze had driven him over the edge.

Three years earlier his drunken yobbery had ended in a disgraceful display of arson and vandalism.

In January 330, Alex and his 60,000-strong army marched into the stunning Persian capital Persepolis.

The city had surrendered without a struggle — on condition its beautiful buildings and temples would not be harmed.

Once inside Alex and his officers began to celebrate with a huge party. As usual, the wine flowed without restraint.

A beautiful Athenian courtesan named Thais, who had accompanied the army into Persia, began teasing Alex.

She grabbed a burning torch from the walls of their huge banqueting hall and dared the king to set the city alight.

Alex, his face flushed with drink, leapt to his feet, grabbed the torch and hurled it onto the roof's wooden rafters.

His officers followed his lead, throwing burning torches all over the building.

Within minutes the hall was ablaze. The fire soon spread across the city.

When the Macedonians marched from Persepolis, the once-beautiful city — the jewel in the Persian king's crown — was nothing but a charred ruin.

Paranoid

As the Macedonian army marched across Asia towards India the heat increased — and so did their thirst.

Water supplies were few and far between so Alex and his men began drinking even more wine to compensate.

The combination of the heat and the constant boozing made Alex increasingly paranoid.

By now the king's boozy parties often went on until dawn.

One morning, as he staggered back to his tent, a crone who claimed to be psychic warned him there was a plot against his life. Alex's pals laughed and said she was crazy but he took her seriously.

Days later the Royal Pages — a group of 15-year-old Macedonian boys who guarded the king's tent — were suddenly arrested.

Under torture a few of the teenagers allegedly confessed to plotting to kill Alex. They were immediately stoned to death.

But that was not the end of the killing. Callisthenes, a Greek philosopher who was the official historian of Alexander's conquests, was also arrested.

He was said to have instigated the Royal Pages' plot. He was tortured and hanged.

Alex's general said last night: "We were all shocked by the plot. Why would a group of 15-year-olds want to assassinate the king?

"It was never explained, but we just accepted it. By that time we had learned that those who questioned Alex's motives often came to a sticky end."

Smart Alex . . . the Macedonian king wears his finest armour and drives a fabulous chariot as he leads the victory procession after his army captures Babylon from the Persians

Art attack . . . an unfinished mosaic of Alex's victory at the battle of Issus

On the run . . . King Darius and his Persian army flee from Alexander's men

DEATH OF A HORSE MADE HIM CRY LIKE A CHILD

ALEXANDER was a ruthless soldier who did not bat an eyelid at terrible slaughter — but he wept like a baby when his favourite horse died.

Alex had owned the horse, called Bucephalas, since he was a teenager and rode it into every battle.

But during a conflict in India it was fatally wounded by a javelin.

Alex was inconsolable over the death of the nag, which was more than 20 years old.

He held a lavish funeral procession in its honour, leading the parade himself.

Tomb

And when he founded a city near the banks of the river where the battle took place he named it Bucephala in the horse's honour.

Bucephalas's remains were laid in a sumptuous tomb built at the centre of the new city.

It is claimed that Alex was the only man who could ride Bucephalas.

In battle the horse was said to be as fierce as its master, biting and kicking out at any enemy who dared to approach.

Horse play . . . a teenage Alex plays with his beloved mount Bucephalas

113,060 DAYS TO GO

The first great Roman road, the Via Appia or Appian Way. Work began on the road, which ran down to the port of Brundisium in heel of Italy, in 312

310 BC

IRON AGE HOMES

IN Iron Age Britain, Celtic families lived either on relatively isolated farms or as part of a small village. Their houses were usually circular and had one room, with different areas for sleeping and cooking.

The walls were made from interwoven branches, usually of ash and hazel.

Over this framework was plastered a sticky mixture of mud, clay and straw. Roofs were usually thatched with straw.

The circular Iron Age house is peculiar to the Celtic tribes that settled in Britain and Ireland. The Celts on the continent generally built rectangular homes.

Most of the British villages were surrounded by a defensive timber wall, sometimes accompanied by a ditch for extra security.

This was a necessary precaution in a society where inter-tribal feuds and raiding were the norm rather than the exception. The warlike nature of Celtic society — and the desire for security — also caused some villagers to build their settlements on artificial islands created in the middle of lakes or rivers.

These villages — known as crannogs — were reachable by a wooden walkway which could be removed like a castle's drawbridge if the tribe came under attack.

Our knowledge of how the Iron Age Celts lived has been boosted in recent years by the experiments at Butser Ancient Farm, near Petersfield, Hants.

A working replica of a Celtic farm has been created there, complete with authentic round houses and the sorts of crops and farm animals that were in use during the late Iron Age.

The experiment has proved that seemingly-flimsy Iron Age homes can withstand hurricane winds and torrential winter rain.

...Timeline...

322 Death of Aristotle; Demosthenes commits suicide. End of democracy in Athens.

321 An entire Roman army surrenders after it is surrounded by the Samnites at battle of Caudine Forks; War between Alexander's generals as each struggles for mastery.

320 Theophrastus begins study of plants.

312 Rome begins building its first great road, the Via Appia, which runs to the seaport of Brundisium in the heel of Italy.

310 Explorer called Pytheas from Massalia (modern-day Marseilles, France) sails around the British isles; Cassander, ruler of Macedonia, executes Alexander's wife Roxanne and son Alexander IV.

A modern reconstruction of a crannog — a fortified Iron Age lake village. The Celts of Britain and Ireland built crannogs to keep out raiders from rival tribes

PYTHEAS THE EXPLORER

LITTLE is known of Pytheas, apart from the fact that he was a Greek sailor and probably a trader from the city of Massalia — modern-day Marseilles in southern France.

Most of the information we do have about his voyage around Britain comes from later Greek and Roman writers who clearly took his claims with a pinch of salt.

Pytheas said he set off from Cadiz and hugged the Spanish and French coasts before crossing the Channel and sailing to Cornwall, where he visited a tin depot at St Michael's Mount. He then sailed around Britain, returning to describe its inhabitants and climate.

Pytheas said the island was triangular and had a perimeter of some 4,000 miles. He claimed the south-east corner was called Kantion — believed to derive from a Celtic word meaning "edge". The name has evolved through the centuries into Kent.

Pytheas also insisted he had voyaged further north and found a previously unknown land which he named Thule.

Historians think this was either Iceland or Norway.

The philosopher Aristotle (top), who died in 322, and (below) the ruins of his Athens school, the Lyceum

A Samnite warrior. The Samnites beat Rome in 321

THE Sun

Friday, September 30, 310BC — **One Coin** — **THOUGHT: HUTTER LUXURY**

GARAGE — **TOILET** — **KITCHEN** — **BEDROOM**

SAIL OF THE CENTURY

I went round Britain in a boat, claims explorer

AN explorer called Pytheas is claiming he has sailed all the way around Britain in a boat.

Pytheas, a Greek from the Mediterranean city of Massalia, said the trip took "quite a few weeks."

He insists he set off from Cornwall, then kept going north until he ran out of land. Then he turned right and followed the coast until he ended up back in Cornwall. Pytheas says he went about 4,000 miles

By LEN D'AHOY

in total and discovered that Britain is shaped like a triangle. If his story is true he will go down as one of the great explorers of this century. But last night there was scepticism about his claims.

One boat expert said: "It's the bit about the triangle that makes me suspicious. Greeks are obsessed with them — that bloke Pythagoras couldn't stop talking about triangles and he was clearly insane."

A Legend In His Own Launch Time — Page Two

...Timeline...

305 Alexander's former generals become kings of their respective territories within his empire — Ptolemy is king of Egypt, Antigonus of most of Asia Minor, Lysimachus of Thrace, Cassander of Macedonia and Seleucus of a vast area stretching from modern-day Iran and Iraq to India, known henceforth as the Seleucid Empire.

301 Antipater dies as his army is defeated by coalition of Alexander's other generals at battle of Ipsus (modern-day Turkey) — his territory is divided up between his rivals Seleucus, Ptolemy and Lysimachus.

300 First lighthouses being built; The first swords begin to appear in Britain.

298 Death of Cassander, king of Macedonia.

295 Euclid develops elements of mathematics.

294 Antigonus's son Demetrius becomes king of Macedonia.

290 Rome emerges victorious from its long struggle with the Samnites — it is now the paramount power in Italy.

288 Birth of Archimedes in Syracuse, Sicily.

285 Lighthouse of Alexandria is finished.

283 Antigonus Gonatas becomes king of Macedonia.

282 Rome becomes embroiled in diplomatic row with southern Italian city of Tarentum after its fleet sails into Tarentine waters. Tarentines sink Roman fleet, then appeal for help to Pyrrhus, king of Epirus — a state which lies just across the Adriatic.

280 Pyrrhus lands in Italy and boasts that he will put an end to Roman interference in southern Italy; He defeats Romans at Heraclea, but suffers heavy casualties; Herophilus, a doctor from Alexandria, Egypt, who was one of the first people to dissect a human body, studies the nervous system and distinguishes between different types of nerve.

279 Pyrrhus again beats Romans at Asculum — his losses are so heavy he famously declares: "Another victory like this and we are lost." The incident gives rise to the ironic phrase "A pyrrhic victory"; Celtic tribe called the Galatians invades Greece.

278 Pyrrhus crosses to Sicily to fight for the Greek cities there against the Carthaginians of north Africa (modern-day Tunisia); Galatians cross into Asia Minor before settling in an area of what is today central and eastern Turkey.

276 Pyrrhus returns to Italy from Sicily.

275 Romans defeat Pyrrhus at battle of Beneventum (southern Italy) — he returns home.

273 Pyrrhus is killed while campaigning in Greece when a woman throws a roof tile which hits him on the head.

269 Rome mints its first silver coins.

266 Roman rule extended to cover whole of central and southern Italy.

264 Start of First Punic war between Rome and Carthage — it breaks out when they support rival warring factions in the Sicilian city of Messana; Roman army moves into Sicily; First gladiatorial show in Rome.

263 Hiero, ruler of Sicilian city of Syracuse, breaks with Carthage to become ally of Rome.

262 Romans capture Sicilian city of Agrigentum.

261 Romans build first fleet of 160 warships — basing them on a captured Carthaginian ship.

260 Aristarchus of Samos estimates moon's size and distance from Earth during lunar eclipse; Archimedes calculates "pi" to two decimal places.

257 Revolt by Parthians, an Iranian people, from the Seleucid empire.

255 Roman army lands in North Africa in a bid to capture city of Carthage — it is decisively defeated at Battle of Bagradas by Carthaginian army.

253 Roman fleet is wrecked off Sicily with massive loss of life.

253 BC

ROME AGAINST CARTHAGE

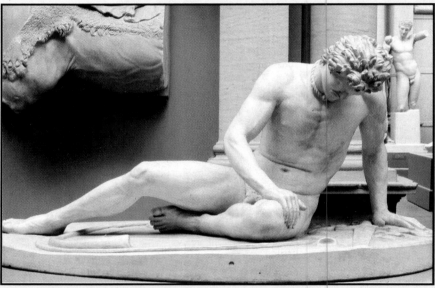

Statue of the so-called Dying Gaul in Rome's Capitoline Museum. Thousands of Gauls served as mercenaries in the Carthaginian armies that fought against Rome

BY the beginning of the 3rd Century BC Rome was the dominant power in Italy. But as its influence spread south towards Sicily it clashed with the other leading power in the region — the north African city of Carthage.

Carthage was founded as a colony of the city of Tyre in modern Lebanon. The Carthaginians were businessmen, using the city's huge navy to build a trading empire in the Mediterranean.

By 300BC it was the wealthiest city in the region, with a population three times that of Rome.

The two cities finally came to blows over Sicily, the jewel in Carthage's empire. Hostilities began after the Sicilian city of Messana (modern-day Messina) appealed to Carthage to send troops to help quell a revolt.

Then the city elders changed their minds and asked the Romans for help instead. Neither Rome nor Carthage would back down and in 264BC war broke out.

The First Punic War, punic being the Roman name for the Carthaginians, lasted 23 years.

Early on the Romans realised they could never win a decisive victory without control of the sea.

So in 260BC they decided to build their first navy — constructing a huge fleet of warships modelled on one captured from the Carthaginians.

Over the next ten years the Romans gradually got to grips with warfare at sea — and inflicted damaging naval defeats on the Carthaginians.

In 255BC the Romans invaded North Africa in a bid to crush Carthage once and for all. But the expedition ended in disaster when their army was utterly defeated in battle.

Worse was to follow. Rome sent a fleet of more than 250 ships to bring the survivors home, but the inexperienced admiral tried to outrun a storm at sea and the entire fleet was wrecked off the coast of Sicily. The loss of life was appalling. Roman historians said more than 100,000 died.

The Roman response was typical. They simply built another fleet, raised another army and carried on. The war dragged on for 15 years more. Finally, in 241BC, Carthage sued for peace. It was forced to quit Sicily, which became a Roman province.

Pyrrhus, invader of Italy in 280, and a Roman warship like those built in 261

THE Sun

Monday, April 5, 253 BC   **One Coin**   **THOUGHT: DUN ROMAN**

Worst sea disaster of all time

Full horrific story: Pages 2, 3, 4, 5 and 6

100,000 DROWN

Nightmare at sea . . . a ship slips beneath the waves with all its crew on board as storm shatters the Roman fleet last night

By MANDY LIFEBOATS

UP to 100,000 Romans were feared drowned last night after an entire navy was destroyed in a terrifying storm at sea.

More than 200 warships were engulfed by the tempest just off the coast of Sicily.

Most of the ships were overturned by the 100mph winds or dashed to pieces against the cliffs.

The soldiers on board, weighed down by armour and shields, never stood a chance once in the water.

WARNING

Last night there were still no signs of any survivors. The tragedy is the worst sea disaster in history.

The navy was heading back to Italy after picking up a Roman army from North Africa following a disastrous campaign against the city of Carthage. Rome is currently in the 12th year of its war against the Carthaginians.

The navy's admiral had **IGNORED** a warning not to set sail. One Roman senator said: "Apparently he was told a storm was coming but decided to make a run for it."

240 BC
GENIUS OF ARCHIMEDES

Archimedes sets light to the Roman ships besieging his home town of Syracuse in Sicily by using mirrors to reflect sunlight on to their decks

ARCHIMEDES is one of the greatest mathematicians ever — and certainly the most famous of ancient Greece. Many of his discoveries were centuries ahead of their time. The Archimedean Screw, a device for raising water from a low to high level, is still used more than 2,000 years later in waste treatment plants.

Archimedes was born in Syracuse, in modern-day Sicily, in 287BC and educated in Alexandria, Egypt. He spent most of his life in Sicily, dedicated to research and experiment.

He is best known for his work calculating the areas and volumes of curved objects and figures, as well as for being the first person to study hydrostatics (the behaviour of fluids and objects immersed in them).

The latter led to the famous, but probably legendary, incident involving Archimedes' bath.

It is said that as he stepped into it, Archimedes realised that the amount of water he displaced exactly equalled the volume of the part of his body which was submerged. It is said that he leapt from the bath and ran down the street naked shouting "Eureka", meaning "I've found it!"

The importance of the discovery was in giving rise to Archimedes' Principle — which states that any object which is completely or partly submerged in a fluid (water, for the sake of argument) is pushed upwards by a force equal to the weight of the fluid it displaces.

Looked at another way, this means that the object loses as much weight as the weight of the water it displaces. A ship lowered into the sea will sink down until the weight of water it displaces equals its own weight. Objects which are denser than water,

and therefore weigh more than the amount of water they displace, sink. Less dense objects float.

Archimedes is once said to have used his Principle to expose a fraud against King Hiero II of Syracuse, who suspected that a new solid gold crown he had ordered was partly made of silver. Archimedes took equal weights

of gold and silver and weighed them in water. In water, of course, they would weigh different amounts because they are of different densities.

Then he weighed the King's new "gold" crown and a replica made from silver, both in water. He was able to compare the results and calculate that the crown was indeed not solid gold.

Perhaps Archimedes' greatest claim to fame, however, is his work with areas and volumes.

In his On The Sphere And Cylinder he was the first person to calculate that the volume of a sphere is two-thirds that of a cylinder into which it will fit exactly. He also calculated that the surface area of a sphere is four times that of its largest circle.

In Measurement Of The Circle he works out pi, the figure by which a circle's diameter is multiplied to calculate its circumference, to be about 3.14 (it's 3.14159265 to eight decimal places).

Archimedes' other great works include Floating Bodies (about hydrostatics), The Sand Reckoner and Spirals. He is said by his contemporaries to have been a great astronomer, though little evidence survives of his findings.

His inventions are of particular note and several of his war machines were used to defend Syracuse from the invading Romans in 213BC.

The most spectacular, though this is possibly legend rather than fact, was a system of mirrors which the city's defenders used to torch the Roman fleet. It is said to have deflected the sun's rays on to the Romans' ships, which were covered with highly-inflammable tar for waterproofing.

Archimedes was killed when the Romans finally took the city in 212BC. Legend has it that when a Roman soldier found him drawing a maths problem in the sand, Archimedes retorted: "Do not disturb my diagrams" and was promptly killed.

...Timeline...

250 Bactrians, Iranians ruled by a Greek dynasty in modern-day Afghanistan, declare independence from Seleucid Empire; Translation of Bible into Greek begun at Alexandria; Ptolemaic expedition begins exploring east Africa; Greek doctor Erasistratus establishes that the heart pumps blood around the body.

249 A Roman fleet is wrecked off coast of Sicily.

247 Carthaginian forces launch new offensive against Romans in Sicily; Arsaces becomes first king of Parthia — Parthians slowly begin encroaching on Seleucid territory.

243 New Roman fleet is built, paid for with voluntary loans from its citizens.

241 First Punic War ends with Roman victory; Carthaginians forced to abandon Sicily to the Romans.

Ruins of the city of Carthage in North Africa, which was defeated by Rome in 241. The Carthaginians fought three wars against Rome — and lost them all

FIRST BIBLE

CHRISTIAN tradition says that the Hebrew Old Testament was first translated into Greek around 250BC at Alexandria, Egypt.

It is known as the Septuagint — an adaptation of the Latin word for 70 — because 70 scholars allegedly carried out the translation.

The work was made up of the first five books of the Old Testament — the Torah of Judaism — which are traditionally said to have been written by Moses.

Egypt's Greek ruler Ptolemy II is reported to have ordered the translation for Jews who had moved to Egypt and could no longer understand Hebrew. It has been suggested that there were so many Jews in Alexandria at this time they made up two-fifths of the population.

In the following centuries further Hebrew scriptures were translated and added to the original five books to make up what the Christian church eventually came to think of as the Old Testament.

THE Sun

Thursday, July 7, 240 BC   One Coin   THOUGHT: AWASH WITH IDEAS

BOLD TESTAMENT

By JENNY SIS

A NEW book that tells a series of old-fashioned tales of adventure, magic and daring has been a surprise smash hit.

The book, The Old Testament, has been selling like hot cakes since it was published in Alexandria, Egypt.

One of its stories tells how a man called Moses uses magic powers to free his friends who are imprisoned by an evil fanatic called Pharaoh. The Old Testament has been a huge hit with kids. One parent said: "It's nice to see that good old-fashioned stories are still popular even in this advanced, modern age."

The Old Testament is available in Greek, though other language versions are planned. A sequel, provisionally titled Old Testament 2, is on the cards.

YOU STREAKER

You silly sud . . . Archimedes leaps from his bath yesterday. He later claimed he had discovered 'something important about water'

Outrage as Archimedes leaps from bath for a naked dash

By KIT OFF

MATHS genius Archimedes caused outrage yesterday by dashing naked through the streets shouting at the top of his voice.

The 47-year-old eccentric shocked neighbours in Syracuse, Sicily, by yelling "Eureka" at them, meaning "I've found it."

He had been in his bath only moments earlier — though last night it was still unclear exactly what he claims to have found in there.

One shocked local said: "I don't care how clever he is or how excited he got in his bath.

FLANNEL

"Grown men do not run down the street without a stitch on in the middle of the afternoon. It's a disgrace - there were women and children around."

Last night Archimedes, famous for his "Screw" device which raises water from a low to high level, tried to calm tension over the incident. He claimed he had made an important maths discovery in the bath which would benefit everyone.

Archimedes said that once he realised the amount of water he displaced when he got in the tub was exactly equal to the volume of that part of his body which was submerged he became so excited he could not contain himself.

But one angry neighbour said: "It sounds like a load of old flannel."

EXCLUSIVE
Volumes, density and me: The Archimedes Story
Only in Sun next week

218 BC

HANNIBAL

A statue of the falcon god Horus at Egypt's Temple of Edfu. Ptolemaic rulers began work on the temple in 237

...Timeline...

240 Eratosthenes of Cyrene, head of library in Alexandria, calculates Earth's diameter with amazing accuracy; First presentation of Greek tragedy and comedy in Latin translation.

238 Sardinia is occupied by Romans; Birth of Philip V of Macedonia.

237 Carthaginians begin to rebuild an empire by expanding into Spain; Ptolemaic rulers of Egypt begin building huge temple of Edfu between Luxor and Aswan.

229 Carthaginians found city of New Carthage (modern Cartagena) in southern Spain.

225 Army of Gauls invades Italy but is defeated by Romans at Battle of Telemon.

223 Antiochus the Great becomes king of vast Seleucid Empire.

221 Hannibal becomes Carthage's commander in Spain and continues expanding its empire; Philip V becomes king of Macedonia; Start of the reign of the Qin dynasty in China; Date of a "battery" found near Baghdad, Iraq, a clay jar with an iron rod surrounded by a copper cylinder — filled with an electrolyte solution such as vinegar it produced about 1.1 volts and may have been used in electroplating.

219 Hannibal lays siege to Spanish city of Saguntum — citizens appeal to Rome for help; Rome sends embassy to Carthage to warn its ruling assembly that it must curb Hannibal or risk war.

Coins issued by Antiochus the Great, ruler of the Seleucid Empire from 223

218 Second Punic War is declared between Rome and Carthage. Hannibal takes the initiative by marching his army from Spain, through southern France, across the Alps and into Italy; He defeats Roman armies at Battles of Trebbia and Ticinus, then continues moving south.

HANNIBAL will be forever associated with the story of his march across the Alps with his war elephants — a feat that sparked the second life-and-death struggle between Rome and the North African city of Carthage.

Hannibal's father Hamilcar had been Carthage's leading general during the first war with Rome. According to legend, when Hannibal was a child, his father made him swear he would never be friends with Rome.

By 220BC Hannibal was Carthage's main general, ruling the city's trading empire in southern Spain — and pushing its boundaries ever outward.

But the Spanish town of Saguntum, just north of modern-day Valencia, did not want to become a Carthaginian outpost and appealed to Rome for help. Rome ordered Hannibal to leave Saguntum alone. He ignored them and in 219BC his troops stormed the town. The next year Rome declared war.

The Romans were confident of a speedy victory and planned to wrap things up quickly by sending one army to Spain, another to North Africa.

But Hannibal struck first. In 218BC the 29-year-old general led a force of some 40,000 Spanish, Gallic and North African mercenaries — along with 37 war elephants — out of Spain and into France.

In early Autumn he made the gruelling crossing of the Alps into Italy. He emerged into Roman territory with an army reduced to 26,000. Many of his elephants had also perished in the mountains. But the audacity of his strategy stunned Rome. The city immediately despatched armies north to deal with the invader.

The first battle on the River Ticinus in Northern Italy was little more than a cavalry skirmish, which the Carthaginians won. In December came the first real conflict at the River Trebbia. There Hannibal lured the 40,000 Roman troops across the river in the early morning mist. As they emerged, he sprung an ambush, attacking them from flank and rear. Only 10,000 Romans escaped.

After a period of resting and recruiting, Hannibal pushed further south. In 217BC he was being pursued by a Roman army led by the general Flaminius.

In April he turned on his pursuers and trapped them in a narrow valley beside the shore of Lake Trasimene in central Italy. The Romans were utterly defeated. Flaminius died with his men.

The victory at Lake Trasimene left the road to Rome open. But Hannibal lacked the equipment for a lengthy siege, so he bypassed Rome and moved into southern Italy in a bid to persuade the cities there to abandon their support for the Romans.

In 216BC the Romans again tried to defeat Hannibal. They raised a vast army, said to number more than 80,000, outnumbering Hannibal almost two-to-one. The battle was fought at Cannae, a small town near Italy's heel.

In the centre, the over-confident Roman infantry pushed forward as Hannibal's troops slowly gave ground. But on the flanks the Carthaginians attacked and beat back the Roman cavalry. Slowly but surely the Roman army was surrounded in a brilliant pincer movement. Only a handful of Roman soldiers survived the butchery.

Cannae was a stunning victory. But ironically it marked the turn of the tide against Carthage. From then on the Romans simply refused to meet Hannibal in open battle, preferring to keep him bottled up in the heel of Italy and starved of supplies and reinforcements. At the same time, Rome's brilliant young general Scipio Africanus was winning a series of victories in Spain.

The great Carthaginian war leader Hannibal

In 209BC he captured the Carthaginians' Spanish capital New Carthage. Within three years Carthage had lost its last footholds in Spain.

In Italy, Hannibal was still a serious menace, but he was in desperate need of reinforcements.

In 207BC Hannibal's brother Hasdrubal led a second army across the Alps into Italy. The two brothers planned to unite and launch a new offensive. But Hasdrubal was intercepted at the River Metaurus in central Italy and defeated. He died in the fighting.

In 204BC Scipio landed with a Roman army in North Africa. The next year Hannibal was recalled to take charge of the defence of Carthage.

In 202BC the final battle of the war was fought at Zama. For hours it was poised on a knife-edge, but finally Scipio's cavalry got the upper hand and Hannibal was defeated.

Carthage surrendered and Rome imposed humiliating peace terms.

In the following years Hannibal took charge of the government of Carthage, bringing in a series of reforms. But Rome still feared him and in 196BC he was forced into exile amid claims he was stirring up trouble.

He spent his remaining years in the service of a variety of monarchs in the eastern Mediterranean. But wherever he went the Romans sought him out. In 182BC he committed suicide at the age of 65 to avoid extradition to Rome.

THE Sun

Thursday, May 29, 218BC   **One Coin**   THOUGHT: EAR THEY COME!

PACK YER TRUNK
WE'RE OFF TO ROME

Elephants take mountain trek

By NELL LEA

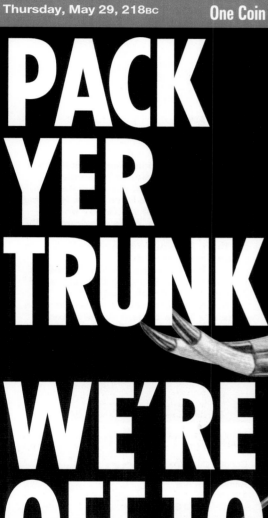

DAREDEVIL soldier Hannibal plans to invade Rome — by marching his war elephants over MOUNTAINS.

Hannibal, 29, has already set out from Spain with 40,000 armed men and nearly 40 of the giant jumbos.

They will cross France, then clamber over the Alps — which are 15,000ft high in places — before storming into Italy.

Once there the Carthaginian leader intends to take on the mighty Roman army and maybe even capture the city itself.

A spokesman for Hannibal said last night: "Obviously there is an element of risk involved — especially for the elephants. But we want to teach the Romans a lesson."

THE TUSK AHEAD: Hannibal writes for The Sun – Page 8

29,138 DAYS TO GO

80 BC

SEVEN WONDERS

MYSTERY surrounds the identity of the first author to compile a list of the Seven Wonders of the ancient world.

Various Greek and Roman commentators are said to have written down their choices of the greatest monuments, but none of these lists has survived.

The Seven Wonders that we commonly refer to today come from a list that was in fact compiled during the Middle Ages.

This lists, in chronological order, The Great Pyramid of Giza in Egypt; the Hanging Gardens of Babylon; the huge Statue of Zeus at Olympia in Greece; The Temple of the goddess Artemis at Ephesus, Turkey; The tomb of King Mausolus, known as the Mausoleum, in Halicarnassus, Turkey; The Colossus of Rhodes, a huge statue of the Sun god Helios; and the Lighthouse of Alexandria, Egypt.

Only the Great Pyramid has survived more or less intact. The ruins of the Temple of Artemis can still be seen, but there are few, if any, remnants of the others.

One of the most intriguing of the wonders is the Hanging Gardens of Babylon, said to have been built around 600BC by King Nebuchadnezzar II, for his wife.

The Hanging Gardens were built close to the river Euphrates in modern-day Iraq. They were allegedly 400ft square and raised about 75ft off the ground by a series of magnificent vaulted arches.

It is said that an abundance of exotic plants grew on the raised terrace of the gardens, many of them trailing over the sides.

One ancient writer said: "The Hanging Garden has plants cultivated above ground level and the roots of the trees are embedded in an upper terrace rather than in the earth.

"The mass is supported on stone columns. Streams of water emerging from elevated sources flow down.

"This is a work of art of royal luxury and its most striking feature is that the labour of cultivation is suspended above the heads of the spectators."

The accounts we have of the Hanging Gardens were all written by ancient Greek historians, none of whom had actually seen them.

There is no mention of the gardens in Babylonian records.

This has led some modern historians to suggest the Hanging Gardens were a figment of Greek imagination.

However, archaeologists working on the site of the ancient city of Babylon have discovered the foundations of a palace which they believe may be the gardens. The evidence is far from conclusive.

...Timeline...

The Rosetta Stone decree (left) of 196, the god Dionysus (centre) whose orgiastic rites were banned in Rome in 186 and a world map dating from 2nd Century BC

217 Hannibal defeats Roman army at Lake Trasimene in central Italy; Romans declare state of emergency.

216 Roman army is crushed by Hannibal at Battle of Cannae; Italian city of Capua goes over to Hannibal.

215 Roman forces sent to Spain launch successful counter offensive against Carthaginian army there; Hannibal occupies southern Italy; Syracuse goes over to Hannibal after death of ruler Hiero; Carthage signs treaty of alliance with Macedonian king Philip V.

214 Romans send army to Sicily under Marcellus — it lays siege to Syracuse, home of Archimedes.

212 Syracuse falls — Archimedes is killed as city is stormed.

211 Romans retake Capua; Roman advances in Spain are wiped out by defeats at the hands of the Carthaginians.

209 New Roman commander in Spain, Scipio Africanus, captures New Carthage.

208 Marcellus killed; Carthaginian general Hasdrubal leaves Spain to link up with Hannibal in Italy.

207 Hasdrubal's army is defeated by Romans at battle of Metauraus in Italy. — Hasdrubal is killed.

206 Scipio ejects last Carthaginian forces from Spain; Start of the reign of Han dynasty in China.

204 Roman senate sends Scipio to North Africa to attack Carthage.

203 Carthaginian assembly recalls Hannibal to defend city.

202 Scipio defeats Hannibal at Battle of Zama; Carthage surrenders.

200 Rome declares war on Philip V of Macedonia and sends fleet and army to Greece; Mathematician Apollonius of Perga names the ellipse, parabola and hyperbola.

197 Macedonians defeated by Romans at battle of Cynoscephalae.

196 Hannibal takes up top political position at Carthage but is forced into exile by Romans; Date of Rosetta Stone decree in Egypt — hieroglyphics with accompanying Greek translation. Its discovery in 1799AD enables scholars to translate Egyptian hieroglyphics for first time.

195 Hannibal joins up with Antiochus.

193 Romans tell Antiochus not to set foot in Europe. He ignores them and invades area around modern Gallipoli in Turkey.

192 Antiochus pushes into Greece. Rome declares war and sends army.

191 Roman forces defeat Antiochus at Thermopylae.

190 Roman army lands in Asia Minor in pursuit of fleeing Antiochus.

189 Antiochus is defeated by Romans at battle of Magnesia; He sues for peace and loses large section of his Asia Minor empire in subsequent treaty.

186 Roman senate passes a law that forbids Bacchanalia — orgiastic rituals in celebration of the god Dionysus.

182 Hannibal, who had fled to Black Sea area, commits suicide after Rome asks for his extradition.

179 Death of Philip V: He is succeeded as King of Macedonia by his son Perseus.

178 Seleucid king Seleucus IV begins persecution of Jews.

173 Rebellion of Jews against Seleucid king, the Maccabaean revolt.

172 Eumenes, ruler of Pergamum, visits Rome and tells senate Perseus is plotting against them.

171 Rome sends army against Perseus.

168 Macedonians defeated at Battle of Pydna, northern Greece; Roman victors abolish Macedonian monarchy.

167 Seleucids massacre Jews in Jerusalem; Temple of Jerusalem rededicated to Zeus.

165 Hydraulic organ built in Alexandria, Egypt; Jewish rebel forces defeat Seleucid army.

164 Seleucid king Antiochus IV halts Jewish persecution.

152 Roman ally Masinissa, king of the Numidian tribesmen of North Africa, raids Carthage.

150 Romans decide to intervene in North Africa on side of Masinissa; First metal coins in Britain.

149 Roman army lands in North Africa and besieges Carthage; Extortion court set up in Rome to try officials who abuse power.

147 Warlike Achaeans of central Greece angry at Rome over its "interference" in Greek politics.

146 Rome declares war on Achaea and invades; Roman army destroys Greek city of Corinth; Carthage is finally stormed and destroyed; A Roman province of North Africa is created.

139 Rebellion of 70,000 slaves in Sicily.

133 Death of last king of Pergamum, Attalus III — he leaves his kingdom to Rome in his will; Roman nobleman Tiberius Gracchus and his brother Gaius begin bid to bring in revolutionary reforms to redistribute land to help Rome's poor — Tiberius is clubbed to death in an anti-reform riot.

132 Romans crush Sicilian slave revolt.

125 Senate refuses to extend rights of Roman citizenship to all Italians.

121 Anti-reform mob murders Gaius Gracchus — 3,000 supporters are executed for treason.

118 Greek historian Polybius dies.

112 Rome declares war of Numidian leader Jugurtha after he seizes throne of North African state.

110 Mithridates, king of state adjoining Black Sea known as Pontus, begins policy of expansion.

106 Birth of Roman statesmen Cicero and Pompey the Great; Jugurtha surrenders to Romans. He is later executed.

105 German tribes who had migrated south to southern France annihilate two Roman armies sent to stop them.

102 Roman general Gaius Marius crushes German army near modern-day Aix-en-Provence in southern France.

101 Marius stops second German army from invading Italy.

100 Birth of Julius Caesar; Paper first used in China; Glass-blowing invented in Syria.

91 Marcus Livius Drusus is assassinated after attempting to pass laws granting Roman citizenship to all Italians — death sparks civil war known as the Social War.

90 Rome suffers setbacks in Social War; Senate halts spread of rebellion by granting citizenship to all Italian cities that remain loyal as well as those prepared to give up.

89 Roman general Sulla wins major victories against Italian rebels.; Political rivalry in Rome between Popular faction, led by Marius, and Conservative faction, led by Sulla; Mithridates declares war on Rome.

88 Sulla leads his army into Rome to force out his rivals; Marius flees Italy. 80,000 Romans and Italians massacred in cities across Asia Minor on orders of Mithridates.

87 Sulla arrives in Greece with army to fight Mithridates; Marius returns to Rome and massacres Sulla's supporters in city; Birth of Roman poet Catallus.

86 Sulla defeats Mithridates army in two battles; Marius dies.

84 All Italians granted Roman citizenship.

83 Sulla lands in Italy with army, sparking civil war in which he is victor.

82 Anti-Sulla Roman senator Sertorius sets up independent state in Spain.

81 Sulla becomes dictator, executing enemies and seizing their property.

THE Sun

Tuesday, October 16, 80BC   One Coin   THOUGHT: PARADISE CITY

WIN
Peter Seabrook's hanging baskets of Babylon
SEE PAGES 20 & 21

GROWING, GROWING GONG

Babylon wins our great '7 Wonders' contest

By OLIVE GROVE

NOW that really IS a bloomin' marvel!

The Sun's sensational Seven Wonders of the World contest has been won by the Hanging Gardens in Babylon, (right.)

Our judges travelled the globe to pick the greatest buildings ever.

And they decided the Hanging Gardens' mixture of exotic shrubs and beautiful brickwork made it Wonder No1.

Our competition has been a huge hit.

But it also sparked a storm last night when it was revealed Britain's Stonehenge had **NOT** made the final shortlist.

Now turn to Pages Four and Five to see the six runners-up.

'WONDERS' CONTEST

Your guide to the world's most magnificent sights

THE waiting's over, folks — an the Hanging Gardens of Babylo have been crowned winner o The Sun's Seven Wonders of the World contest.

But there are six other building that came close to sneaking the title And here, we're giving you a guide

2 Pharos

THE Pharos — or Lighthouse — in the harbour at Alexandria is the most modern of the Wonders.

Work was begun on the lighthouse by Egyptian king Ptolemy the Saviour — a friend of Alexander the Great — in 290BC. He wanted to help sailors find their way safely back to port in an area where hidden rocks made the sea treacherous.

The lighthouse works by using a giant mirror which reflects the sun's rays during the day — and the light of a fire by night.

Sailors say the reflection can be seen some 35 miles off shore. It is believed to be one of the tallest buildings in the world, reaching the seemingly impossible height of 300ft.

3 Pyramid

THE Great Pyramid at Giza was built by the Egyptian pharaoh Khufu in about 2560BC — making it the oldest of The Sun's Seven Wonders.

Amazingly, the ground-breaking pointed building was not constructed as a palace — but a tomb.

It took thousands of slaves and workmen more than 20 years to finish the pyramid, which is made of almost two million blocks of stone.

Khufu was eventually buried in the heart of the pyramid in a coffin of red granite. Nearby was buried a boat which was supposed to transport the Pharaoh to the next world.

The pyramid is even taller than the Pharos of Alexandria — reaching almost 480ft. Each of the four sides of the pyramid measure 751ft.

4 Tomb of Mausolus

THE tomb of King Mausolus is a stunning white marble and gold building that was constructed by his wife Artemisia.

It took two years to build and was finished in 351BC.

The burial chamber itself is set on top of a 60ft high podium.

The edges of this are decorated with a series of stunning life-size statues of people, lions, horses and other animals.

The burial chamber features a selec-tion of Greek-style stone columns which hold up a triangular roof. At the point of the roof sits a gigantic statue of a man in a chariot pulled by four horses.

The total height of the tomb is about 140ft.

Mausolus ruled the area of Asia Minor called Caria. He was known as a satrap — a minor ruler who came under the overall command of the king of Persia. In his later years he took part in a revolt against his overlord — but wisely changed sides when he realised the rebellion was doomed to fail. Luckily for him, he was forgiven and allowed to retain control of his kingdom.

Although the tomb was planned by Mausolus, the work was actually begun by Artemisia — who was his sister as well as his wife — and completed a year after her death.

The magnificent sculptures are said to be the works of four leading art-ists from Greece.

The two architects are also thought to have been Greek.

THE 6 RUNNERS-UP

By EDDIE FISS

tour of the unlucky runners-up. In second place came the amazing Pharos or Lighthouse of Alexandria, a shining beacon of modern architecture.

The famous Great Pyramid of Giza claims third place.

The oldest of the Seven Wonders, it was the bookies' hot favourite to land the title. In fourth place is yet another tomb — the magnificent burial place of King Mausolus in Halicarnassus, Asia Minor.

We knew we'd never stop the Greeks winning a prize, so it's no surprise to see the magnificent Temple of Artemis at Ephesus taking fifth place. Number six is the first of two prize-winners to feature a giant figure — the Colossus of Rhodes, one of our ancient world's top tourist attractions.

And last, but by no means least, at number seven is the amazing gold statue of Zeus at Olympia.

As in all Sun competitions, the Editor's decision is final. No correspondence will be entered into.

6 Colossus

THE Colossus of Rhodes — the giant statue of the Sun god Helios that towered over the harbour of the Greek island — is currently lying on the floor!

Work was begun on the 110ft bronze figure in 304BC and took 12 years to complete.

But just 56 years later the isle was rocked by an earthquake and the statue snapped off at the knees, its weakest point.

It is still lying where it fell today. But The Sun judges were assured plans are afoot to repair it and so decided to award it sixth place.

The judges' spokesman said: "We thought it was too magnificent to ignore — even if it is broken at the moment!"

5 Temple of Artemis

THE huge Temple of Artemis at Ephesus is the finest example of Greek architecture, The Sun's judges decided.

The panel reckoned it is even **BETTER** than the magnificent Parthenon in Athens — and that takes some beating.

The temple — which features more than 127 columns — is thought to have been built about 550BC in honour of Artemis.

She is the goddess of hunting and nature that the Romans call Diana. The marble building is said to have been funded by the Lydian king Croesus — whose name has become a byword for immense wealth — and designed by the famous Greek architect Chersiphron.

Like the Tomb of Mausolus, it too was decorated with a series of sculptures, many of them bronze, from the finest Greek artists.

The temple is one of the most popular tourist sites in the Mediterranean world — many of its thousands of visitors leave small statuettes of the goddess as a tribute to her.

In 356BC a crazed vandal tried to burn the temple to the ground — because he said he wanted to become famous.

According to legend Alexander the Great was born on the same night — and the goddess ignored the blaze because she was looking after him.

The resulting fire did serious damage, which took more than 20 years to repair. Alexander himself later paid for further repairs.

7 Zeus

THE fabulous gold statue of Zeus at Olympia was created by the famous Greek sculptor Pheidias.

He made the statue by sculpting a number of different parts and assembling them inside the Temple of Zeus. The finished figure stands about 40ft high — and almost touches the Temple ceiling.

One tourist guide says of the magnificent figure: "On his head is a sculpted wreath of olive sprays. His sandals are made of gold, as is his robe. His garments are carved with animals and with lilies. The throne is decorated with gold, precious stones, ebony and ivory."

But Pheidias has been criticised for making the statue too big for the temple. One critic said: "It looks like he's going to bump his head."

72 BC

ANCIENT CHARIOTS

THE chariot was invented around 1700BC and quickly became the most important weapon in the ancient armies of the Assyrians, Egyptians and Hittites.

But their importance declined after the Assyrians began to introduce large numbers of true cavalrymen into their armies about 700BC.

By the 1st Century BC the Romans used chariots only for racing or in processions. Few armies still used them, with two notable exceptions. The army of the eastern king Mithridates, who ruled a kingdom on the shores of the Black Sea called Pontus, featured large chariots with sharp metal scythes protruding from their wheel hubs.

In theory, the chariots, pulled by four large horses, would drive at speed into the massed ranks of the enemy, its scythes causing huge casualties.

In practice, though, the chariots were extremely unstable and the slightest unevenness in the ground caused them to turn over. If they did manage to stay upright, the driver would dive to safety when the chariot was still yards from the enemy.

This left no one to steer, so enemy soldiers would merely open their ranks to leave a gap which the chariot horses would gallop through harmlessly.

A second exception was found in Britain. In the 1st Century BC, a lighter, more mobile, two-horse chariot was still used in large numbers by the Celtic tribes here. The Celts of mainland Europe had long since abandoned the chariot for the horse, but the Brits proved more conservative.

Julius Caesar, in his account of his expeditions to Britain in 55 and 54BC, remarked on how skilfully the Britons handled these chariots, which were light enough for a man to carry.

In the 1970s archaeologists at a late Iron Age site at Gussage All Saints in Dorset found the remains of what is believed to be a Celtic chariot-making factory dedicated to the large-scale production of the war vehicles.

LIFE OF SPARTACUS

SPARTACUS was born in Thrace (modern Bulgaria) and served for a spell in the Roman army before deserting. He was captured and sold as a slave to a gladiatorial training school in Capua, southern Italy.

In 73BC he and a group of other gladiators escaped and formed themselves into an army. They were joined by huge numbers of runaway slaves, said by the Romans to number almost 90,000. For two years Spartacus and his army looted and pillaged across Italy, defeating five Roman armies sent to stop them.

Finally, in 71 BC, the Roman general Marcus Crassus crushed the rebel army in battle. Spartacus himself was among the dead. The rebels who survived were crucified.

SNETTISHAM TREASURE

THE priceless collection of Celtic jewellery known as the Snettisham Treasure was found buried in a field in Snettisham, Norfolk, between 1948 and 1990. It consists of more than 150 gold, silver and bronze necklaces plus many coins. Scholars think it may be the royal treasure of the Iceni tribe that ruled East Anglia in the 1st Century BC.

Gold Celtic necklaces, known as torques, from the Snettisham Treasure (also far left)

...Timeline...

79 Sulla gives up dictatorship after enacting series of reforms and retires to his country estates; Sertorius defeats Roman army sent to regain control of Spain.

77 Pompey sent to Spain.

74 Mithridates defeats Roman army in Bithynia (northern Turkey); Roman senate orders new offensive against pirates in the eastern Mediterranean.

73 Slave revolt led by Spartacus breaks out in Italian city of Capua.

72 Roman navy defeated by pirates off Crete. Spartacus defeats Roman forces. Sertorius is murdered by an aide and Pompey regains control of Spain for Rome; Estimated date of the Snettisham Treasure — a hoard of Celtic gold and coins found buried in a Norfolk field and possibly buried by the wealthy rulers of the Iceni tribe of East Anglia.

Hollywood's Kirk Douglas stars in the epic 1960 movie Spartacus. The historical Spartacus, a gladiator, was the leader of a rebellion against Rome that began in 73. His army of renegade gladiators and runaway slaves, said to number 90,000, terrorised Italy for two years before the rebellion was crushed by the general Marcus Crassus

THE Sun

Thursday, February 2, 72BC   **One Coin**   **THOUGHT: CART-ASTOPHE**

WOADSAMONEY
Norfolk tribe buries hoard of gold -SEE PAGE 20

SPARTACURSE

SPARTACURSE

From RON AMOK in Rome

A SLAVE named Spartacus had the mighty Romans quaking in their beds last night after he gave their soldiers a severe beating.

Spartacus and his army of 90,000 slaves and gladiators ambushed a huge Roman force which was sent to crush their rebellion.

Witnesses to the battle in central Italy claim only a few hundred Roman soldiers escaped.

Spartacus, 29, was a gladiator at the famous training school in Capua, Italy, until he and his fellow fighters rioted last year.

They fled into the surrounding countryside and were soon joined by thousands of runaway slaves. Spartacus then

Rome threatened by humble slave

formed the men into a huge army. Yesterday's victory marked the THIRD time in nine months the slaves have defeated a Roman army.

And last night there was panic on Rome's streets as rumours spread that Spartacus and his followers now intend to march on the city.

Citizen Timor Mortis said: "I've sent my family to stay with relatives in Sicily — and I'll be following them soon."

CHARIOTS OF FIRED
5 jobs go as plant closes

The popular new Middle Eastern chariots have sharp scythes, fancy paint jobs and power to spare

FLASH

Traditional British chariots are pulled by two ponies and do not accelerate as fast as foreign models

TRASH

EXCLUSIVE

By JAY LOPPY

BRITAIN'S best-known chariot factory is to close for good at the end of the month.

The entire workforce of **FIVE** will get the boot when the MG Chariots plant shuts.

A spokesman for the 60-year-old firm said: "It's a sad day for the British chariot industry."

SLICED

MG Chariots, based in Gussage All Saints, Dorset, was once among the leading war vehicle makers in the world.

But it has increasingly been losing out to the flashier, faster models produced in the chariot factories of the Middle East.

Most of these boast four horse-power and custom paint jobs. Partic-

ularly popular are the models with sharp metal scythes on the wheels – designed to slice up enemy warriors who get too close.

In recent years, the Brits hit back by unveiling their sporty new MG Woadster model.

This had a revolutionary wicker body which made it much lighter than previous chariots.

But it was still only two horse-power – and had an alarming tendency to turn over if drivers took a corner too fast.

Giddy Upp – editor of chariot racing magazine Whoa! – said last night: "The Brit models are just too slow. All today's tribesmen want to drive a flashy foreign beast."

Wicked Joyriders Scythed Me Down
— Pages Eight and Nine

ROMAN COOKERY SPECIAL

Mousewatering

You'll love tasty rodent treat

FED-up with serving your tribesman the same boring old meals when he climbs from his chariot after a hard day's farming?

Then why not give him a treat by cooking one of the great new Roman dishes that everyone's talking about?

After all, what could be more mouthwatering than dormouse cooked in honey or roasted sow's belly? Yum!

Below we've given you a couple of recipes to get you started. The first, roast flamingo, is a real family favourite in Rome. The second, fish sauce, is used to spice up many meals — try it poured over pork chops!

Once you've tried these you'll probably get the taste for Roman cuisine, so we've given you a sample menu, just in case you invite a couple of friends round for a light lunch. Don't forget, you'll need plenty of wine with the food.

Most of the ingredients used in Rome are easily available throughout Britain.

However, sometimes it can be a little difficult to get hold of fresh flamingo. If you have trouble, a large parrot makes a very good substitute.

Tasty . . . honey is used to sweeten dishes

Treat . . . belly of sow is Roman favourite

Filling . . . a roast boar makes a fab snack

RECIPE ONE

ROAST FLAMINGO

1 Take two flamingos. Pluck, wash and truss the birds, put in a pan and roast over a strong fire.

2 Add water, dill, a dash of vinegar, chopped leek and coriander.

3 Pound some pepper, cumin, coriander, mint and basil. Moisten the mixture with a little vinegar.

4 Add some dates to the mixture and pour the stock from the cooking flamingos over it to make a tasty sauce.

5 Thicken the sauce with a little flour, then pour over the flamingos. Serve with vegetables.

Light Latin lunch menu for 4

Gustatio (Starters)
White and black olives
Damsons and pomegranate seeds
Dormice sprinkled with honey and poppy seeds
Grilled sausages with fish sauce
Honeyed wine

Fercula (Main course)
Roast fattened flamingo, sow's belly, roast whole wild boar served with dates and stuffed with live thrushes, boiled whole pig stuffed with sausage and black puddings. Serve with 100-year-old Falernian wine

Mensae secundae (Dessert)
Fruits and cakes
Boned, fattened chickens and goose eggs
Pastries stuffed with raisins and nuts
Quince apples and pork
Oysters and scallops
Snails

RECIPE TWO

FISH SAUCE

1 Catch a selection of small oily fish, like sprats, anchovies or mackerel. Mix them all together and place on a large stone baking tray.

2 Add two pints of salt to the fish. Mix well, making sure the salt is rubbed into all the fish.

3 Leave overnight, then transfer to an earthenware pot. Place outside for three months, stirring mixture regularly with a stick.

4 Take pot from garden, cover with lid and store in a dark, warm place. Once a week, skim liquid scum from surface of pot's contents and use as fish sauce.

Garrius BUSHELLUS

We came for blood and gore ... we got a no-score bore

THE ROAR of the crowd, the splash of blood, the crash of iron on iron . . . nothing in our beloved Rome can match the thrill and spectacle of the amphitheatre.

Last night two mighty champions stepped out in to the freezing dusk, pledging to fight on until one of them died (of embarrassment).

This, as no one ever said of Keithius Chegwinus, was the big one.

Antonius Blair, trained by Lurkio Mandelson, versus Hagus The Barbarian.

If Antonius won, he pledged to swear allegiance to a new Caesar and sell the true Brits into slavery in Germania and Gaul.

For his part, Hagus The Barbarian was promising his supporters an independent groat and half-price rides in his chariot.

Sluts

Escorted out into the arena by a luscious, full-lipped hairy Goth (Naughtius Portillo, also known as Ben Duh) Hagus immediately dazzled the crowd — by lowering his head.

Antonius was seconds behind him, carried aloft by his supporters Brutus Campbell and Kennus the Red who seemed to have accidentally stuck his knife in his back.

Immediately flaming arrows began to pierce the icy air. "That'll teach Emperor Kinnockius not to seat the Women's Institute so close to Antonius's corner," whispered Hagus.

"Coo-ee my Emperor," shouted his handmaiden Ffffion.

"How do you know me?" asked Kinnockius.

"I've seen your bust," said Ffffion.

"Show me yours and I'll be merciful," replied the Emperor. But his words were drowned out by the sound of well-drilled legionaries marching forward to begin the pre-fight ritual of sacrificing virgin slave-girls before him.

"Why do they sacrifice virgins?" asked Antonius.

"Well," said Brutus, "they're not going to get shot of the sluts."

The entertainment over, the two champions began to circle each other. Then they circled again.

Onions

For three long weeks they ignored the catcalls of a bored crowd (Henghis Pod and his wife Senna) as they tried to knock each other out with a killer combination of hot air and A-level name-calling.

Then Antonius snapped. "Release the fox!" he cried. "But don't kill it."

Hagus froze. He knew his opponent was a shrewd tactician. He remembered the mess he'd made of John Major-Domo, the grey-haired Tory sage who never really knew his onions.

"Unleash the British Lion," cried Hagus.

Entertainer Julius Clary entered the arena.

"I said 'LION', not Iron," said Hagus in exasperation.

But it was too late. The crowd walked out and so did I.

...Timeline...

71 Mithridates defeated by Roman general Lucullus — he takes refuge with son-in-law Tigranes, the king of Armenia; Roman general Marcus Crassus defeats Spartacus — his 20,000 followers are crucified, but he is thought to have died in battle and his body is never found.

70 Tigranes refuses to hand over Mithridates to Romans; Cicero prosecutes Roman governor of Sicily for extortion; Roman poet Virgil, author of The Aeneid, is born.

69 Lucullus invades Armenia and defeats its army — Armenian king Tigranes surrenders but Mithridates escapes and fights on.

68 Mutiny in Lucullus's army in Asia Minor over his strict discipline.

67 Pompey given special mission to stamp out pirates from Eastern Mediterranean — he clears the area of them in a brilliant three-month campaign on land and sea.

66 Pompey takes over from Lucullus in Asia Minor — he defeats Mithridates, who flees before committing suicide.

65 Roman poet Horace is born in southern Italy.

64 Pompey campaigns in Asia minor, capturing Syria and Jerusalem; End of Seleucid kingdom.

63 Cicero unmasks plot by senator Cataline to overthrow government and seize power — plotters are later executed; Birth of Gaius Octavius, the future emperor Augustus; Pompey reorganises Asia Minor states — whole of Middle East and North Africa is now made up of Roman provinces or puppet kingdoms; Romans invent a form of shorthand.

62 Greek historian Diodorus Siculus reports how Egyptian mob lynched a Roman for killing a cat — Egyptians, who believed cats to be sacred, often placed them in temples and even had them mummified when they died.

61 Julius Caesar is made governor of Spain — his first major political appointment.

60 Caesar returns to Rome; He joins with Pompey and wealthy businessman Marcus Crassus in a secret alliance to promote each other's political ambitions — The pact is known as the First Triumvirate.

59 Pompey seals pact with Caesar by marrying his daughter Julia; Birth of historian Livy — best known for his History of Rome.

58 Cicero is exiled by political enemy on trumped-up charges of having illegally executed the traitor Catiline and his co-conspirators; Caesar begins military campaigns in Gaul (modern-day France) by attacking a tribe of migrating Gauls called the Helvetii.

57 Cicero returns to Rome in triumph after exile order is overturned; Street fighting in Rome between mobs supporting rival Popular and Senatorial political factions.

An Egyptian mummified cat (top) and Pompey, who allied with Caesar in 60

56 BC

WEAPONS OF WAR

IN the ancient world developments in weapons technology were few and far between. By the beginning of the 1st Century BC the Roman army had become Europe's dominant military force.

The backbone of it was the legionary who was armed with a short stabbing sword — the gladius hispaniensis or Spanish sword — and a couple of heavy javelins.

He fought shoulder to shoulder with his comrades in a formation traditionally made up of three lines.

The legionary was supported by lighter-armed foot troops, usually archers, slingers and javelin throwers.

Similarly, cavalrymen would be armed with javelins and swords. Only the semi-nomadic Parthians who dominated the area of modern-day Iraq used mounted bowmen to any significant degree.

Turn the clock back 700 years and you will find the Assyrian armies that conquered much of the Middle East using similar javelins and swords and firing similar bows.

But what was relatively new was the widespread use of war engines — giant catapults made of wood that could hurl large stones or arrows. The prototype catapults were invented by the Greeks around 350BC and later adapted and improved by the Romans.

The machines fired their missiles using springs made from twisted strips of animal sinew.

They were primarily used during sieges to batter walls or shower defenders with missiles.

The Romans occasionally mounted them on horse-drawn carts so they could be more easily moved around and therefore used in open battle.

By the late 1st Century BC each Roman legion probably included its own catapult unit.

The Romans called the stone-throwing machine a ballista. The arrow-firing machine was called a scorpion. During the Christian era the Romans developed a larger stone-throwing machine which was known as the Onager, or Wild Ass.

BRITISH COINS

THE earliest British coins, found in Kent, date to some time before 100BC. They are not thought to have been minted here, but instead brought in from Gaul, possibly as payment in some trade agreement.

On one side they show a man with a beard, on the other a horse and chariot.

By about 80BC many of the tribes in southern Britain had begun producing their own coins — copying closely the styles used by their Celtic relatives on the continent.

At first they were a mix of bronze and tin but gold and silver ones soon followed.

These usually featured human heads, stalks of wheat, horses or chariots.

The so-called Spanish sword that was used by Roman troops, and an officer's plumed helmet

THE Sun

Monday, September 1, 56BC   **One Coin**   **THOUGHT: FLINGS LOOK BAD**

Top Gun

Throwing down a challenge . . . one of the new Roman catapults ready to fire at a walled town

EVIL ROMANS WILL BRING SECRET WEAPON WITH THEM

THIS is the awesome secret weapon that the wicked Romans plan to use when they try to invade Britain next year.

The device, which is called a catapult, can hurl large stones or giant arrows long distances.

It is designed to let the cow-

By TERRY FYING

ardly Roman army batter down the walls of towns without having to get too close.

The Romans have already used the machine with great success across Europe.

Their top general Julius Caesar, who is planning to invade Britain next year, is said to be a big fan.

Last night a spokesman for

the British Army branded the new weapons "unsporting" — and vowed not to copy them.

He added: "What's wrong with the traditional idea of warriors slaughtering each other face to face?

"I think resorting to this sort of long-distance stone-throwing simply proves the Romans are scared of getting hurt."

20 Ways To Decapitate A Roman — Page 15

BRITS SHUN EURO COINS

Gold money 'too flashy to spend'

By PENNY DREADFUL City Editor

THE controversial new Euro-style coins have been a huge FLOP, The Sun can reveal.

Tribal leaders in the south of Britain brought in the flashy new gold and silver coins to replace the traditional bronze ones.

But locals are refusing to use the money — based on coins that are widely used over the Channel in Gaul — because they reckon it is too valuable.

Now instead of buying their vegetables and chariot wheels with the new cash, they are hoarding it.

One tribesman said last night: "I've got hold of a few of these new coins and I won't be parting with them. I'm planning to keep mine safe by burying them in the back garden."

A source among the Atrebates tribe of southern Britain confessed that there was now a severe shortage of money.

He said: "It's been a financial disaster. We'll either have to reissue the old coins or start bartering."

● WANNA get your hands on some ready cash? We've got THREE of these great new coins to give away. Turn to Page 23.

15,861 DAYS TO GO

44 BC

JULIUS CAESAR

JULIUS Caesar is probably the most famous Roman of all. He was born in July 100BC into an aristocratic family fallen on hard times.

From his earliest years he was determined to succeed in the murky world of Roman politics.

Caesar spent the first 20 years of his adult life in a series of minor political and military posts. Then, in 61BC, he was made Roman governor of Spain.

On his return to Rome a year later he formed an alliance with Rome's two leading men, the general Pompey and the rich businessman Crassus.

The three pledged to help each other's careers. The link was further strengthened when Pompey married Julia, Caesar's only child. In 59BC Caesar was elected to be one of the two annual consuls, the magistrates who effectively ran the Roman republic.

But the bully-boy tactics used by Caesar's supporters during the elections caused uproar. There were calls for his prosecution, but Pompey and Crassus used their influence to get Caesar appointed governor of Gaul.

At that time, the Roman province of Gaul covered only a small part of southern France. But during the next eight years Caesar launched a series of relentless military campaigns that brought the whole of France, Belgium, Holland and parts of Germany under Roman control.

In 55 and 54BC he launched expeditions to Britain. These missions were not serious attempts at invasion and on both occasions he returned to Gaul after only a few weeks.

The military conquests won Caesar fame. During the campaigns he also amassed a vast fortune in loot.

After Crassus was killed on a military expedition in 53BC relations became increasingly strained between Pompey and Caesar.

To make matters worse, the senators in Rome backed Pompey in a bid to get rid of Caesar once and for all. In 49BC the Senate told Caesar to quit his army in Gaul and return to Rome.

Caesar realised he faced arrest if he obeyed, so he led his army into Italy — starting a civil war. Pompey was ill-prepared for it and had to flee Italy with his supporters. Caesar pursued them to Greece, where he defeated Pompey in battle. Pompey fled to Egypt, only to be murdered by aides of King Ptolemy XIII.

Caesar arrived soon afterwards and met the king's sister Cleopatra.

The two became lovers and Cleopatra had a son, Caesarion, by Caesar. He appointed her joint ruler of Egypt.

In the following years Caesar mopped up the last of his opponents in Africa and Spain before returning to Rome in 45BC as sole ruler of a huge empire. But his enemies, a group of 60 senators led by Cassius and Brutus, were not yet vanquished.

On March 15, 44BC — known as the Ides of March — they struck. Caesar was stabbed 23 times as he arrived for a meeting of the senate and fell dying beneath a statue of Pompey.

Julius Caesar is stabbed to death (left) by his enemies in 44. The picture is from a 1970 movie. On the right, Caesar accepts surrender of Gallic tribal chief Vercingetorix, who in 52 led rebellion against Rome

...Timeline...

55 Caesar lands in Britain. After defeating a British army he returns to Gaul.

54 Caesar's second invasion of Britain; Rebellion in Gallic areas conquered by Caesar; Death of Julia, wife of Pompey and daughter of Caesar.

53 Annual elections in Rome scrapped because of rioting; Rebellion in Gaul put down; Crassus is killed when Roman army he is leading is almost wiped out at battle of Carrhae (in eastern Turkey) during an expedition against the Parthians; Pompey and Caesar become enemies.

52 New revolt in Gaul sparked by tribal leader Vercingetorix, who surrenders after a siege at the Gallic town of Alesia.

51 Parthians invade Roman province of Syria; Caesar crushes revolt in Gaul; Caesar's opponents at Rome launch series of attacks on him in Senate.

50 Ultra-conservative faction in Senate calls on Pompey to "save the state" from Caesar by taking over command of all Rome's armies; Caesar marches into Italy with his army — sparking civil war.

49 Pompey arrives in Greece to muster his forces.

48 Caesar's army crosses to Greece and he defeats Pompey at the battle of Pharsalus; Pompey flees to Egypt, where he is killed by aides of Ptolemy XIII, who wants to win Caesar's backing; Caesar arrives in Egypt.

47 Senate appoints Caesar dictator with Mark Antony as his deputy; Ptolemy XIII dies and Caesar sets up Cleopatra and her brother Ptolemy XIV as joint rulers of Egypt; Cleopatra gives birth to Caesar's son, Caesarion.

46 Caesar arrives in North Africa and defeats enemies there; He returns to Rome and reforms calendar; Cleopatra arrives in Rome.

45 Caesar arrives in Spain — defeats last of his enemies at Battle of Munda; Civil war ends.

44 Plotters, led by Brutus and Cassius, stab Caesar to death in Rome; Cleopatra returns to Egypt.

Coins issued by Caesar after he was appointed dictator in 47

THE Sun

Wednesday, March 16, 44BC   One Gold Coin   THOUGHT: BRUTE FORCE

THEY CAME, THEY SAW, THEY CONK-ERED

Why a Roman loves to stick his nose in other people's business - Special Report, Page 6

ROME'S WORST NIGHTMARE

OH NO THEY'VE KILLED CAESAR!

From GAY PING-WOUND in Rome

IDES OF MARCH EXCLUSIVE

ROME was in turmoil last night after dictator Julius Caesar was knifed to death.

Caesar, 65, was stabbed more than 20 times as he walked into a meeting with senators. He died instantly.

The assassins are believed to be a group of disenchanted republican politicians led by Brutus and Cassius.

It is thought they feared Caesar was on the point of making himself king after sena-tors granted him almost total control over Rome's vast empire.

Last night the murder looked set to plunge Rome into another terrible civil war as rival factions battle for power. Among those expected to try to seize control is Caesar's trusted aide Mark Antony.

Caesar's adopted son, 19-year-old Octa-vian, is also said to be keen to rule. But a Senate insider said last night: "He stands no chance — he's too young."

Who Was This Caesar Geezer? — Page Seven

Two cavalrymen from the Parthian army. The Parthians, who had an empire based in modern-day Iran, invaded Syria in 40 but were pushed back by Romans

...Timeline...

Marcus Brutus, ringleader of the plot to kill Caesar, committed suicide in 42 after his army was defeated by forces of Mark Antony and Octavian at battle of Philippi

43 Mark Antony, Octavian and Caesar's aide Lepidus agree to rule Rome together in a group known as the Second Triumvirate; More than 2,000 of their enemies are executed — among them are Cicero, who had rashly criticised Antony in a number of speeches.

42 Brutus and Cassius commit suicide after their army is defeated by that of Mark Antony and Octavian at the battle of Philippi. Senate makes a Caesar a god.

41 Antony leaves Rome to tour the east, but spends winter in Egypt with Cleopatra.

40 Parthians invade Syria but are defeated by Romans. Cleopatra has twins by Antony. Antony, Octavian and Lepidus meet to divide up the Roman world between them. Antony gets the East, Octavian the West and Lepidus gets Africa. Antony seals pact by marrying Octavian's sister Octavia.

38 Antony and Octavia spend winter in Athens. She bears him a daughter.

37 Antony abandons Octavia and returns to Cleopatra. He marries Cleopatra despite being still wed to Octavia.

37 BC

ANTONY & CLEOPATRA

THE tale of the Roman general Mark Antony and the Egyptian queen Cleopatra is one of the enduring love stories of history.

But beneath the heroic myth of doomed love is a more sober tale of politics and treachery.

After the assassination of Caesar in 44BC Rome was plunged into civil war. Three of Caesar's men emerged victorious — his deputy Mark Antony, his adopted son Octavian and his trusted aide Lepidus.

In 40BC they divided the vast Roman territories between them. Octavian was to get Gaul, Italy and Spain. Antony would get Asia Minor, Greece and Egypt. Lepidus would get Africa. The deal left Lepidus as the junior partner — the real power lay with Antony and Octavian.

Antony was about 40. He was an able general and a gifted speaker. But he often drank to excess and could be dangerously impulsive.

Octavian, just 19 when Caesar was murdered, lacked Antony's charm and military skill but was cool, calculating and a brilliant politician.

The two men sealed their alliance with a wedding — Antony marrying Octavian's sister Octavia.

However, Antony was already deeply embroiled with Cleopatra. He had met the Egyptian queen, who was of Greek descent, during a tour of Rome's eastern provinces.

The couple spent the winter of 41BC in Alexandria. The following year the 32-year-old queen had twins by Antony.

Nevertheless, Antony and Octavia spent the winter of 38BC together in Athens and she bore him a daughter.

The next year Antony abandoned Octavia and returned to Cleopatra. To add insult to injury he married the Egyptian queen, despite being still wed to Octavia.

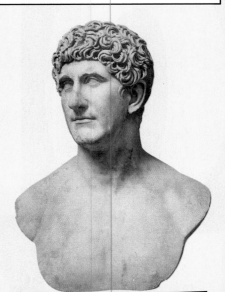

A bust of Mark Antony (top) and an Egyptian carving of Cleopatra (below)

Antony's behaviour outraged the conservative Romans. Their fury was stirred up by Octavian, who said Antony intended to hand over Roman territories to the foreign queen.

In 36BC the balance of power began to swing against Antony. As Cleopatra gave birth to his third child he launched a military expedition against the powerful Parthian empire which covered much of Asia. It was a disaster from the outset and the humiliated Antony had to retreat.

By contrast Octavian easily crushed an attempted rebellion by Lepidus and took over his territories.

In 32BC Antony divorced Octavia. War was now inevitable and Antony and Octavian both moved their armies and navies to bases in Greece.

At the beginning of September 31BC Octavian's gifted general Agrippa decisively defeated Antony and Cleopatra's navy at the Battle of Actium. The lovers managed to escape back to Egypt, but their navy and army surrendered.

Six months later, as Octavian's troops reached the outskirts of Cleopatra's capital Alexandria, she withdrew to a sumptuous stone tomb with a fortune in jewels and gold. Here she planned to receive Octavian and attempt to buy her freedom.

When Antony heard Cleopatra was in the tomb he presumed she planned to kill herself. He decided to follow her lead and thrust his sword into his stomach. He was near death when a messenger arrived urging him to join Cleopatra and meet Octavian.

Antony's servants carried him to Cleopatra and he died in her arms.

Later that day Octavian's men burst into the tomb and grabbed Cleopatra They took her back to her palace, where she was placed under arrest.

A few days later Cleopatra's maids smuggled in a nest of poisonous snakes hidden among a basket of figs. The queen, fearing Octavian planned to parade her though the streets of Rome in triumph, allowed the snakes to bite her, fatally.

LOVERS
Picture that proves Antony is carrying on with Cleo

EXCLUSIVE

ROYAL temptress Cleopatra lets her hands Rome over hunky general Mark Antony — in a picture that PROVES the pair are lovers.

The Egyptian queen and the handsome Roman have been insisting for months that they are just good friends.

And Antony claimed only last week that he was staying at Cleo's fabulous palace in Alexandria to discuss a treaty between Egypt and Rome.

But this exclusive picture shows that his relations with the sultry monarch are more than just diplomatic.

The revelation will be a bitter blow to 43-year-old Antony's aristocratic wife Octavia. The couple have been married for less than three years and she recently gave birth to his daughter. A

From YVES DROPPER in Alexandria

pal said last night: "Octavia will be absolutely heartbroken.

"She trusted Antony when he said he had to go to Egypt on a business trip. He has betrayed her."

Antony first met 34-year-old Cleo, an unmarried mum of three, while he was on a tour of duty in the eastern Mediterranean with the Roman army.

TORRID

They became friends and were regularly seen out on the town. Gossips have claimed the twins she later gave birth to were his. Insiders say Antony may now divorce Octavia and wed Cleo.

The queen is certainly no stranger to scandal involving Roman generals.

She had a torrid fling with Antony's pal Julius Caesar and later gave birth to his son Caesarion.

Picture by LEN SCAPON

MOST GLAMOROUS COUPLE IN WORLD: Pages 4 & 5

We're on a stroll . . . Antony and Cleo wander in Alexandria

Wild pair who love to party

ANTONY and Cleopatra have become famous for throwing some of the most extravagant parties ever.

Guests, who are served on solid gold plates, eat the most exotic foods and drink vintage wines. At one banquet the cooks were ordered to roast more than 20 wild boar — to feed just a DOZEN revellers.

Cleo threw one of the most lavish bashes when she first met Antony.

She invited him to party on her private barge, which was completely covered in gold.

The boat's sails were purple, while the oars were made of silver. To top it all, Cleo sat in the middle of the boat —

dressed as Aphrodite, goddess of love.

Later the couple threw a sumptuous bash in Alexandria to celebrate her birthday.

Both she and Antony showered gold and gems on the visitors. A Greek partygoer called Plutarch said afterwards: "It was amazing.

"Many of those who arrived as paupers left as rich men."

Cleo and Antony both love practical jokes.

They regularly dress up as servants or slaves and wander around Alexandria.

Antony got in a row with a citizen while in disguise — and was punched for being "a cheeky slave."

Pud up job . . . waiters serve dessert at one of Cleo's banquets

POSH 'N PECS

From RANDI ROYALE in Alexandria

ANTONY and Cleopatra are the king and queen of the showbiz world — living a glamorous lifestyle that other stars can only dream of.

Cleo, nicknamed Posh because of her Royal background, was recently voted the Middle-East's sexiest monarch — beating rivals like the Queen of Sheba, Helen of Troy and Nefertiti.

Antony, dubbed Pecs because of his muscular physique, has been Rome's top pin-up boy for years.

As a couple they are a match made in heaven — and people do not seem able to get enough of them.

They are rarely off the front pages of the newspapers — and the glossy Roman showbiz magazine Hail! is said to have paid a fortune for exclusive pictures of them relaxing in Cleo's lovely Egyptian palace.

Paparazzi

Hail! Editor, May Kitupp, said last night: "Without doubt Antony and Cleo are hot stuff at the moment.

"For months they have been insisting that they are just friends — but no one was fooled.

"They were constantly seen riding around in a flash racing chariot.

"And the paparazzi managed to do umpteen paintings of Antony and Cleo emerging from banquets arm in arm."

The first signs of a romance came shortly after they met three years ago.

The Sun revealed how Antony had suddenly taken an interest in fashion — clearly prompted by the clothes-conscious Queen of the Nile.

Sun Fashion Editor Gloria Mundi said: "Up until then Antony had been very conservative in dress — standard-issue Roman battle tunic, plain armour, things like that.

"Suddenly he was wearing gilded breastplates decorated with little cherubs, thigh-high sandals and brightly-coloured wrap-around skirts."

A few months later stunning brunette Cleo gave birth to twins — a boy and a girl — which were rumoured to be Antony's.

Gossips said the tough Roman had even had the word Alexandria tattooed on his back — to remind him of where the kids had been conceived.

There were changes in hairstyle too. Antony suddenly abandoned his military pudding-bowl cut for a daring new look.

Tongues

This was a dyed-blond crop with the words AMOR VINCIT — Latin for Love Rules — carved into the back.

But his dalliance in Egypt soon got him in hot water back in Rome.

Trouble flared when he failed to turn up for a military training session, designed to get the army fit before the start of the campaigning season.

Antony claimed he could not get away because Cleopatra's children were ill — and he needed to help run the country while she nursed them.

But reports leaked back to Rome that the pair had been seen knocking back wine at a party to launch the Egyptian edition of Caesar's memoirs.

The senators were furious — and axed Antony as general for a cam-

paign against the German tribesman. The dropping of the star general caused uproar in Rome. Antony was accused of putting a foreign floozie before the interests of the empire.

The only way he could save his career was by marrying Octavia, the strait-laced sister of Caesar's adopted son Octavian.

Antony tried to make a go of his marriage, but he longed to be with Cleo and soon left for the East, saying he was going on a business trip.

Within weeks he was back in Alexandria with the queen. It's not the

Queen Cleo and Roman beefcake are world's most glam couple

They're departying . . . chariot waits to drive Mark and Cleo home from rave-u

first time Cleo has caused tongues to wag in Rome.

A few years ago she managed to seduce Julius Caesar himself when he visited Egypt.

She stunned the great general by hiding herself in a carpet which was unrolled in front of him.

When the scantily-clad beauty went tumbling across the floor Caesar was said to have gasped in delight.

Later, after leaving Egypt to return to Rome, he told pals: "I've never enjoyed myself so much since I divided Gaul into three parts."

special

swordsman . . . hunky Mark Antony is Rome's leading pin-up

Saucy of the Nile . . . stunning
Cleopatra shows off the sexy
figure that has wowed Antony

1,229 DAYS TO GO

Cleopatra commits suicide inside her palace in Alexandria in 30. Her lover Mark Antony had already killed himself

...Timeline...

36 Antony launches expedition against Parthia — but is forced to retreat; Cleopatra has Antony's third child; Octavian makes Lepidus retire and takes his territories.

32 Octavia, sister of Octavian, divorced by Antony.

31 Octavian's general Agrippa defeats Antony and Cleopatra in the sea battle of Actium.

30 Antony commits suicide in Alexandria; Cleopatra also kills herself shortly after Octavian and his army enter Alexandria; Egypt is annexed by Rome.

29 Octavian undertakes ambitious rebuilding programme in Rome.

27 Octavian reforms Rome's constitution to effectively make himself ruler of the Roman world and its first emperor — adopting the name Augustus.

21 Agrippa marries Augustus's daughter Julia.

20 Three tribes become dominant in southern Britain — the Catuvellauni, controlling Hertfordshire and north of the Thames, the Atrebates in Hampshire, Berkshire, Surrey and Sussex and the Trinovantes in Essex.

19 Death of Roman poet Virgil, author of the Aeneid.

13 Work begins on Augustus's Altar of Peace in Rome.

12 Death of Agrippa; Augustus becomes Pontifex Maximus, chief priest of Rome.

8 Death of poet Horace, famous for his Satires and Odes.

6 Augustus's stepson Tiberius gets a share of his step-father's power.

Augustus's Altar of Peace in Rome. The monument, which was begun in 13, was intended to remind Romans the emperor had put an end to decades of civil war

3 BC

BODY IN THE BOG

The remains of the so-called Lindow Man in fact lay undiscovered for nearly 2,000 years. On August 1, 1984, two men digging peat from a bog in Lindow, Cheshire, found what appeared to be the remains of a human foot.

They alerted police, who soon found the upper half of a human body. Scientists discovered it was that of a man who died some time after 5BC.

The upper part of the body had been perfectly preserved by the peat. And while scholars called him Lindow Man, he earned the nickname Pete Marsh because of the spot where he was found.

A detailed examination suggested that Lindow Man did not die from natural causes but was probably the victim of a ritual murder, possibly involving the druids.

He was well-built, 5ft 7ins and about 30. His skull had been fractured and he had been strangled with a rope made of animal sinews. His jugular vein was cut, possibly to drain the blood from his body. After death he was thrown naked into a shallow pool. The ritual killing theory was strengthened when his stomach was found to contain the pollen of misletoe, a plant sacred to the druids, and burned pieces of biscuit.

Historians believe the burned biscuit fragments may show that Lindow Man was the sacrificial victim at the Celtic festival of Beltain, held on May 1 and intended to ensure crops grew.

As part of the ceremony a small portion of a biscuit was burned, then placed in a bag with a number of unburned pieces.

The worshipper who picked the burned fragment from the bag had the "honour" of being sacrificed.

Lindow Man's hair had been neatly trimmed just before his death and his nails were well manicured, signs suggesting he was from a well-to-do sector of society.

Remains of a fox-fur armband — a symbol of the Celtic nobility — were also found at the site, suggesting that "Pete" may even have been a prince or king.

SCANDAL IN ROME

JULIA, daughter of Rome's first emperor Augustus, was at the centre of one of the great scandals of the ancient world. She was 27 and a widow twice over when in 11BC she was forced by her father to marry the future emperor Tiberius.

The couple were said to be happy at first, but soon became estranged.

According to Roman historians, Julia used the separation as an excuse to conduct a series of scandalous affairs with prominent Romans.

Augustus was a strict moralist and had passed a series of laws that punished adulterous wives with execution.

But no one had the courage to tell him how Julia, a mother of five who was famous for her beauty, was behaving. According to the law, Tiberius had a duty to reveal his wife's cheating. But Julia was Augustus's favourite and Tiberius feared that he would place his own life in peril by denouncing her.

Eventually Livia, Tiberius's mother and Augustus's second wife, secured proof of her step-daughter's adultery and presented the facts to her husband. Augustus was furious, but was unwilling to execute his daughter — banishing her in 2BC to a tiny island instead.

When Tiberius became emperor on Augustus's death in 14AD he refused to pardon Julia, who died in exile within a year.

ANCIENT CLOCKS

THE ancients used two methods to tell the time — sun dials and water clocks. The Ancient Egyptians are thought to have begun building tall pillars known as obelisks to use as primitive sun dials as early as 3500BC.

By 1500BC they were using shadow clocks — sundials with hours marked on them.

In later centuries sundials became more elaborate and sophisticated. At the end of the 1st Century BC, one Roman writer claimed there were at least 13 different styles in use. Water clocks were usually bowl-shaped stone devices into which water dripped at a regular rate.

Markings on the inside of the bowl measured the passage of time.

The earliest water clock was found in the tomb of the Egyptian ruler Amenhotep I, who died around 1500BC.

The Greeks began using them around 350BC, calling the devices clepsydras, or water thieves.

More ingenious water clocks were developed after 100BC by Greek and Roman astronomers.

THE Sun

Monday, August 17, 3BC

One Coin

THOUGHT: TOFF LUCK

Julia . . . roaming in Rome

ROME IS ROCKED BY SEX SCANDAL

By WANDA INGHANS

A HUGE sex scandal involving the Roman Emperor Augustus's stunning daughter Julia erupted last night.

A private investigator is said to have compiled a dossier detailing the scandalous behaviour of Julia, 36.

It claims she has had flings with scores of men since she married Augustus's stepson Tiberius six years ago.

A source said last night: "This really is hot stuff — the woman is out of control.

"The dossier is very detailed and proves Julia has been entertaining men from every sector of society, from senator to street cleaner."

Tiberius, 39, has been away from Rome on official business for the past three years.

Harsh

But the report claims that he fled the city because he was humiliated by his wife's shameful behaviour.

Julia's antics will stun 60-year-old Augustus, who dotes on his witty and talented daughter.

The emperor passed strict morality laws recently which introduced harsh penalties for adultery. The most serious offenders face the death sentence.

Augustus's wife Livia is believed to have hired the investigator to spy on Julia, the emperor's daughter from his first marriage.

She hates Julia because of the way she has treated her son.

Julia has been married twice before. She and Tiberius have no children, but she has three boys and two girls from her previous marriages.

Thrown into a bog, his throat slashed, his skull crushed. Could this be missing Prince Pete?

By VIOLET DEATH, Crime Correspondent

A MANGLED body found in a bog was last night feared to be that of missing Prince Pete Marsh.

The man's corpse was discovered by workers digging in a peat bog in the north of Britain.

An examination of the body showed he was probably murdered. He had been strangled and his skull smashed.

There were also signs that his throat had been slashed, possibly after he was dead.

Speculation was growing last night that the remains are those of Prince Pete — a nobleman from the Brigantes tribe who has been missing for six months.

SINISTER

Pete, 31, stormed out of his home after a row with his family over his plans to become a druid.

The sinister cult was recently banned on the continent over claims that it sacrifices humans in its bizarre rituals.

A druid spokesman last night denied the cult had anything to do with Pete's death. He said: "We rarely go in for human sacrifice. It's very old-fashioned."

Some Day My Prince Will Come: Pete's Wife Talks To The Sun — Pages 4 & 5

Pete . . . vanished after bust-up

1   DAY TO GO

1BC

THE COMING OF CHRIST

Above, spectacular painting by Nicolaes Berchem (1656AD) of the angel appearing to the shepherds as they watched their flocks to tell them of Christ's birth. The painting on the right, by Octave Penguilly-L'Haridon (1863AD) shows them hurrying to Bethlehem on the angel's advice to see the Messiah for themselves

ACCORDING to Christian tradition, the birth of Jesus Christ was heralded by the appearance of an unnaturally bright star.

The New Testament tells how it led the three wise men of the east to Christ's birth place.

Matthew's Gospel says the three followed the star until they reached Bethlehem.

Once there they paid homage to Jesus and gave him gifts of gold, frankincense and myrrh.

The New Testament begins the story of Christ's coming by telling how the angel Gabriel visited a young woman living in the Galilee town of Nazareth to explain she was going to have God's son.

The angel told her: "Do not be afraid, Mary. God loves you dearly. You are going to be the mother of a son and you will call him Jesus. He will be great and will be known as the Son of the most high."

Luke's Gospel says Mary, who was engaged to a carpenter called Joseph, was terrified — but said: "I belong to the Lord, body and soul. Let it happen as you say."

Later, when Mary was due to give birth, she and Joseph had to go to Bethlehem to take part in a census ordered by the Romans.

The town was so packed they were unable to find lodgings anywhere and had to sleep in a stable.

Luke tells how, as Mary was giving birth there, an angel of the Lord appeared to shepherds who were out in the fields guarding their flocks. The angel said Christ the Saviour had been born. He said that if the shepherds went to Bethlehem and looked in the stable at the inn there, they would see for themselves. The shepherds went straight to Bethlehem and found Mary, Joseph and the baby exactly as the angel had predicted.

The Christian religion teaches that the birth marks the arrival of the Messiah — the redeemer who will save Mankind.

The word messiah itself is an English translation of a Hebrew term meaning "the anointed one".

To the ancient Hebrews, anointing a person with oil meant that they were qualified to play a significant religious role in the community. In the earlier books of the Old Testament, the priests, prophets and kings of the Hebrews are all referred to as messiahs at different points. But by the 1st Century BC the term had come to represent the future ruler of the Jews whose coming had been prophesied.

Many thought this meant a political saviour who would rescue the Jews from the oppression of Roman rule.

Christian tradition claims there are more than 300 prophecies in the books of the Old Testament that prove Jesus was the longed-for Messiah.

Many are said to relate to his descent from Abraham, Isaac and King David.

The Book of Isaiah is said to refer to him being born of a virgin, rejected by his own people — and eventually executed among criminals.

...Timeline...

2 Augustus exiles daughter Julia, wife of Tiberius, from Rome because of her scandalous behaviour; Britain's population estimated to have been 3.5million to 4million at this time — far in excess of the 1.5million recorded in the Domesday Book of 1086AD.

Above, Augustus (2BC) — also on lighter coins, left. Darker ones depict Herod, Galilee's ruler from 4BC

THE Sun

Saturday, December 24, 1BC   One Coin   THOUGHT: OF GOD

Index

Index

Acknowledgements

THANKS TO: Phil Leach, for bringing the ideas to life once again, to Steve Lewis for some fantastic, imaginative photos, mum-of-one Holly Whitelaw for the avalanche of pictures, Emma Holder, Sean Clark, Saul Salmon and Dean O'Brien for their page-building skills and ideas, Sun columnists Garry Bushell and Ally Ross for humouring us, Kathryn George and Roy Cooper for the graphics, Dave Gaskill for his cartoon and Ted Andrews for the Rockmobile, Deidre's Photo Cavebook and the Hebrew doorway.

Immense gratitude to Jon Hughes at Bedrock Studios (of Walking With Dinosaurs fame) for making the front and back cover ideas a reality.

A special mention too for Phil Gregory and The Sun's Imaging Department for their creativity as much as for their hard work.

Thanks also to Myles Archibald, Clare Mercer and Philip Parker at HarperCollins, to Jack and Tineke Perry for the Scrolls For Schools picture and to Janet Smy for the index.

Honourable mentions for other Sun staff: Roger Crump (for the reporter's picture on the covers), Becky Goddard, Katy Lygoe, the Systems, Art, Page-Building and News SubEditing departments and the Picture Desk. Also to Russell Dewey on the Pairing Desk once again. We are indebted to the following for supplying pictures: AKG Photo; The American Museum of Natural History; Anthony Blake Photo Library; Ancient Art and Architecture Collection; Angus McBride; Ardea London Ltd; The Art Archive; Associated Press; The BBC Natural History Unit; The Bridgeman Art Library; British Museum, Werner Forman Archive; Bruce Coleman Collection; Butser Ancient Farm; Capital Pictures; Chrysalis Picture Library; Corbis; Dinamation; Dorling Kindersley; Dover Museum, Kent; English Heritage; e.t. archive; The Fine Art Photographic Library; The Fortean Picture Library; Gallica; Getty One; Girandon; The Granger Collection; Greenhill Books/Peter Connolly; J.C. Allen; The Kobal Collection; Kurt Suleski; Mary Evans Picture Library; Montvert Publications; Moviestore; Museum of London; Natural History Museum, London; NHPA; Osprey Books; Oxford Scientific Films; Premaphotos Wildlife; The Ronald Grant Archive; Salamander Books; Scala Group; Science Museum/Science and Society Picture Library; Science Photo Library; Tony Stone Images; World Pictures.

DEDICATED TO TONY, NORMA, ALISON, ELAINE AND JAYNE.

THE Sun

THANKS A LOT, FOLKS!